Blessings
From The
Shepherd

Blessings
From The
Shepherd

EVELYN GOFF

Charleston, SC
www.PalmettoPublishing.com

Blessings From The Shepherd

Copyright © 2020 by Evelyn Goff

All rights reserved

No portion of this book may be reproduced, stored in a retrieval system, or transmitted in any form by any means–electronic, mechanical, photocopy, recording, or other–except for brief quotations in printed reviews, without prior permission of the author.

First Edition

Paperback ISBN: 978-1-64990-915-2
eBook ISBN: 978-1-64990-569-7

Table of Contents

Chapter 1. Living the Blessed Life 1

Chapter 2. The Shepherd 9

Chapter 3. Where the Shepherd Leads 19

Chapter 4. My Sheep Know My Voice 27

Chapter 5. Blessed by Obedience 35

Chapter 6. Commitment 41

Chapter 7. In the Shepherd I Will Trust 49

Chapter 8. Blessings From the Pit 57

Chapter 9. Blessed Today 69

Chapter 10. One Moment With the Shepherd 81

Chapter 11. In His Presence 91

Chapter 12. The Broken Veil 99

CHAPTER 1
Living the Blessed Life

Perched upon some magnificent island, listening to the sound of waves crashing upon the seashore may sound like your perfect world. Or perhaps living large on your luxurious yacht as you float along the top of the ocean waters or drifting down a river stream seems like the life of your dreams. Maybe a countryside setting with a home nestled underneath the shade of a big sprawling tree is more your style. Lounging on your porch, sipping your morning cup of coffee, listening to the chirping birds as you feel a nice breeze blowing in the wind may sound cozy and inviting. Possibly a charming house, surrounded by a white picket fence, located in a busy neighborhood, bustling with activities, seems like the perfect setting for your family. Of course, plenty of money rolling in makes this dream seem a little sweeter. But, my friend, the blessed life that Jesus Christ desires to give you far exceeds the place where you live or the amount of your portfolio.

Blessings of the Lord are not dependent upon your prestige, power, or wealth. His blessings rain down upon the healthy and the sickly, the rich and the poor.

Whether you reside in a fancy mansion or live in a shack, His blessings can find you wherever you may be. You may live a blessed life regardless of your social status or influence. Instead of flowing out of your basket, real blessings flow from the hand of the Shepherd.

The power and honor of His majesty, and His untold riches are more than sufficient to abundantly bless you. His voice was powerful enough to speak the entire world into existence. In the midst of a storm, howling winds must bow at His command. He calmed the raging seas merely by speaking the words, *"Peace, be still."* (Mark 4:39) Child of God, He has spoken blessings into your life. By His authority, you are blessed. *"For You, O Lord, will bless the righteous; With favor You will surround him as with a shield."* (Psalm 5:12) You move, live, and breathe because of His greatness, not your own.

Out of His abundance of wealth, you are blessed. *"And my God shall supply all your need according to His riches in glory by Christ Jesus."* (Philippians 4:19) Riches untold, which cannot be measured by the standards of this world, belong to Him. If you could measure all the glorious splendor of heaven, then you could measure the abundance of His great riches. Flowing from His throne are bountiful blessings that could never be purchased with silver or gold.

Worthy, worthy, to receive all honor and praise. One day every knee shall bow before Him. Every mouth shall confess Him as Lord. Imagine the entire human race bowing, recognizing Him as the King of Kings and the Lord of Lords. No one on earth deserves the honor that He is so worthy to receive. Upon the honor of His majestic name, every promise that He has made will be fulfilled. Upon the authority of His name, reach out and receive His blessings.

Neither higher position of honor, nor greater reign of authority could ever be found than that of Jesus Christ, the Son of God. Backed by all the authority of heaven, He took on the form of man. He came to this earth to die a cruel death. His death was the only means of restoring the broken relationship between God and man that had been caused by sin. How blessed we are that He came!

Eternal life, the most grand and glorious blessing of all, is granted to every born-again believer. *"For God so loved the world that He gave His only begotten Son, that whoever believes in Him should not perish but have everlasting life."* (John 3:16) Awaiting you is a beautiful mansion that has been paid for in full. The street of your new neighborhood is paved with pure gold. Forever there will be a continual flow of the purest, crystal clear water that you ever saw. Along the riverbank stands a tree, like no other, bearing the fruit called life. Never again will you be plagued with tears, sorrows, or pain. Forever your heart shall overflow with unspeakable joy, peace beyond comprehension, and indescribable love. Satisfaction and contentment like you have never known before lie before you. The blessings of the Lord will never cease.

But, what about now? Do I wait until I see the pearly white gates to enjoy a blessed life? Of course, the blessings of this life cannot compare to the blessing of heaven. But, by all means, He came to give you a blessed life here and now. Blessings come in many different ways. Through unexpected means, blessings may come knocking on your door. The Lord is surely the source of all your blessings, regardless of the means in which they arrive.

Misery loves company. Knowing that he has been defeated, Satan is a miserable foe. Destroying your joy, happiness, fulfillment, and ultimately your life is his delight. Creating a mess in your life, as well as everyone else in the world, is His goal. Never fear, a greater force than he, Jesus Christ, has come to cancel out the wicked plans of the enemy. *"The thief does not come except to steal, and to kill, and to destroy. I have come that they may have life, and that they may have it more abundantly."* (John 10:10) While the enemy plots to destroy and kill you, the plans of Christ are to bless you immensely. Most assuredly, the devil has come to stress, oppress, and depress you. But Jesus came to bless you. Emphatically, Jesus Christ, your Savior, Redeemer, Deliverer, the Almighty Victorious One, came to give you a life that is overflowing with love, joy, and peace. His mercy and Grace, flowing abundantly into your life, is supreme above all.

Abundant life does not mean problem free living. Trials always have a way of weaving into our lives. *"My brethren, count it all joy when you fall into various trials."* (James 1:2) Since James said "when" instead of "if," you fall into trials, then trying times must be inevitable. Face your trials with confidence in the Lord. His sustaining Grace will carry you to the other side. You shall not face one trial alone. The Lord will go before you, behind you, and surround you. Surrounded by His glory in every situation of life shall be comforting to your soul.

Nothing about a bush full of thorns is appealing to the eye. But, oh, how the appearance changes when a few little buds of roses begin popping up. When those buds become fully blossomed roses, that thorny bush has become a gorgeous sight. You may look upon the dull, barren, thorny bush with anticipation of the beauty that it will produce. Such is life. Trials may not look so pretty, nor feel so good, but some of your greatest blessings may lie on the other side.

Paul suffered from a thorn. Although Paul asked three times for the thorn to be removed, he endured the thorn for the remainder of his life. In spite of the thorn, by the Grace of God, he lived an abundant life. Paul discovered the beauty on the other side of the thorn. Not looking to his circumstances, his hope was found in Christ. Like Paul, we can live a blessed life, in spite of the trials that come our way.

Jesus Christ, the Good Shepherd, who never takes His eyes off of the sparrows, surely keeps an ever-watchful eye upon you. For the sake of the world, His own life, He did not spare. *"I am the good shepherd. The good shepherd gives His life for the sheep."* (John 10:11) Many are the sheep that are in His pasture, but He cares for you as if you were His only little lamb. *"Know that the Lord, He is God: it is He who has made us, and not we ourselves. We are His people and the sheep of His pasture."* (Psalm 100:3) While tending to His flock of millions upon millions, He lovingly seeks you out. You are one voice in the midst of a multitude, calling upon His name. Yet, He hears you speak, as if you were the only bleating voice. Your every teardrop comes before Him as if you were the only one who ever shed a tear. His full, undivided attention is turned toward you. Giving such undivided attention to countless people is only possible to Him.

A pasture full of one hundred sheep. Daily the shepherd counts—one, two, three—and the count continues to one hundred. All one hundred sheep safely in the fold brings a sigh of relief to the shepherd. But one day, the count only goes to ninety-nine. What do you suppose the shepherd would do? The Good Shepherd, Jesus Christ, would go searching for the one little, lost lamb. Finding the one wayward lamb is cause for a joyful celebration.

A little baby lamb, unable to walk on my own that is who I am. Incapable of meeting my own daily needs, I need a helping hand. Too blind to see all the pitfalls before me, I need someone to guide me. Unwise choices, I surely will make. I need someone to smooth out the rough roads that I may take. Walking along beside me, the Shepherd takes my hand, helping me to stand. Then step-by-step, I walk in His strength. My daily needs, He does supply. Gently, He guides me along life's journey. He picks me up each time that I stumble. Then, I take a deep breath, and relax in His loving arms.

Your greatest treasures are not in the houses or land that you possess. The place of your earthly dwelling, vacations taken, or millions in the bank will never satisfy the heart like the Shepherd desires to satisfy your every longing. Being in His sheepfold, living in His pasture, is living the blessed life.

CHAPTER 2

The Shepherd

"The Lord is my Shepherd; I shall not want. He makes me to lie down in green pastures; He leads me beside the still waters. He restores my soul; He leads me in the paths of righteousness For His name's sake. Yea, though I walk through the valley of the shadow of death, I will fear no evil; For You are with me; Your rod and Your staff, they comfort me. You prepare a table before me in the presence of my enemies; You anoint my head with oil; My cup runs over. Surely goodness and mercy shall follow me All the days of my life; And I will dwell in the house of the Lord Forever." (Psalm 23)

Making Him your Lord makes Him your Shepherd. "Hear, hear all you sinners! Repent and come into the sheepfold," is the cry of the Shepherd's heart. Surely, He would not accept me, some may say. But oh, how wrong you are! No sin that you have committed is too big, too ugly, or too disgusting that He will not forgive. The stain of every sin, His blood will wash away, making you white as snow. *"Come now, and let us reason together, says The Lord, Though your sins are like scarlet, they shall be white as snow; though they are red like crimson, they shall be as wool."* (Isaiah 1:18) Watching the snow as it falls to the ground, whether glittering underneath the rays of sunlight or sparkling on a moonlit night, may just be the purest form of white that mortal eyes have ever seen. Jesus will cleanse your darkest sins to the most magnificent, purest white imaginable.

Neither, your greatest accomplishments, your best efforts, nor your good deeds can wash away your sins. Religion does not open the gate into His sheepfold. The gate swings open wide to those who have been cleansed by the washing of His blood. Walk through the gate, then you may enjoy a holy, divine, personal relationship with Jesus Christ. The moment that your sins are washed away is your most blessed moment of life.

Great blessings He bestows upon His sheep! Always looking out for their best interest, His sheep shall not lack any good thing. The world has no heavenly gifts to offer. Coming down from above are the most wondrous gifts of all. *"Every good gift and every perfect gift is from above, and comes down from the Father of lights, with whom there is no variation or shadow of turning."* (James 1:17) Relationship with Him is the greatest of all His gifts. Nonetheless, He is ever mindful of the needs that we have in this life.

Wandering through the wilderness, ravaged with hunger, the Israelites were miraculously blessed with food from above. A taste of heaven, a sweet little wafer called manna, rained down upon them each morning. Amazingly, a huge flock of quail flew into the camp each day, providing meat for them. A heavenly feast was generously provided day by day. With no water in sight anywhere, they became parched with thirst. Just as God did not forget them in their hunger, He did not forsake them in their thirst. "Strike the rock with your rod," God commanded Moses. Sure enough, water came gushing out of the rock as Moses obeyed the Lord. God graciously provided all that they needed during the forty-year journey. Amazingly, even their clothes and sandals did not wear out throughout the entire trip. Forty years wandering in a wilderness, and they suffered no lack.

You may never walk outside your door and see manna falling out of the sky. You may never strike a rock and be supplied with water. You may be provided with a job, along with the strength, skills, and abilities for the task at hand. Unexpected resources may come your way, blessing the socks off of you. Although He has not promised to meet all your wants, He has promised that you shall not be in lack. His providential care looks after you the same as it did the Israelites.

At times, His sheep may become tired and weary. But then, He tenderly leads them to a luscious green pasture. The color green signifies life. Dead grass, trees, or any other plant life is never decorated in the vibrant color of green. The once beautiful green foliage turns into a dull brown as life fades away. Resting in the serenity of the green pasture, His presence hovers over you, refreshing your soul.

Soil enriched with life-giving nutrients will surely produce lively green pastures. Immersing yourself in His presence enriches the very core of your spiritual life. Adding fertilizer to the seed is the study of His Word. Like a good, soaking rain, prayer waters the spiritual seed that has been planted in your heart. The more time that you spend with Him, the greener the grass grows. Time spent in the green pasture is a time of worship unto Him and restoration to your soul.

Worry, anxiousness, and fear will lead you away from the green pasture and into a field of dead weeds. Worries and woes rumbling through your mind will have you wallowing in a field of tumbleweeds instead of a green pasture of rest. Sorry, but you probably will not solve any of your woes while tumbling in the field of tumbleweeds. *"Be anxious for nothing, but in everything by prayer and supplication, with thanksgiving, let your requests be made known to God."* (Philippians 4:6) In other words, get out of the tumbleweed patch and down to the green pasture.

Gently, He leads His sheep by a stream of refreshing still waters. Sheep will not drink from troubled, rushing waters. The stream is a place where you may lay all your burdens down. This is a place where your blues can be washed away. Freely, you may come to the river and find satisfaction in your soul. Sitting quietly on the bank of the still waters, reflecting upon His goodness, embellished in His presence, is like a breath of fresh air.

On the outside, you may look like a beautiful picture, with all the pieces of life perfectly put together. But on the inside, you feel beaten and tattered into a million pieces. The front that you put up may fool other people. We probably all have been guilty of smiling through our pain, pretending that all is well. But all our pretense has never one time fooled God. This is a perfect time to enjoy a trip to the green pasture and the refreshing stream of water. In all of your busyness, don't run past the lively green pasture nor skip along the refreshing stream of water for a quick splash. Take time to lie down and soak in His presence for a little while. You will arise feeling refreshed and renewed.

All hope is renewed as your soul is rejuvenated. In your weakness, you are now made strong. In those times of refreshing in the Lord, doubts are erased, and your faith soars to new heights. Confidence is restored so that you may boldly come before His throne. Many slumped shoulders have been made straight, and heads that hung low have been lifted high as a trip was made to the green pasture and the still waters.

You shall not create your own path. Never steering you wrong, the path that He leads you upon will always be right. His sheep never stumble upon the righteous path by happenstance. The Holy Spirit is the guide, leading the sheep to the path of righteousness. The Word of God is the compass used by the Holy Spirit, pointing toward the road called righteousness. *"Your word is a lamp to my feet And a light to my path."* (Psalm 119:105) The Holy Spirit will help you to know the truth. Blessed is the path in which He leads.

Rebellious sheep that kick and stomp, refusing to follow Him to the green pasture and the serene stream of water, probably will not follow Him onto the righteous path either. Rebellion takes one down a long and winding road that eventually ends at an intersection called heartache and grief. Repentance is the U-turn in the road, leading onto a peaceful avenue.

Life is not always lived in the green pasture and down by a nice, quiet stream. Troubled waters will come your way. Rest assured, His blessed presence will be with you as you walk through your most fierce dangers. Though the enemy would hurl vicious attacks your way, you have nothing to fear. Unknown are the times that the fierce, roaring lion was ready to attack, when just in the nick of time, the Shepherd came along beside you, defending you against the evil predator.

You shall not be overcome by fear as you walk through the valley of the shadow of death. The valley shall not become your dwelling place, rather a passageway. You shall not get stranded and stay in the valley; you will walk through to the other side. Remember that a valley is only a ravine between two mountains. When you go through the low spots of life, look ahead—the Shepherd is leading you to higher ground.

You could be beaten to death with a club, but the shadow of the club cannot harm you. You could be mangled for life by a car hitting you, but never could the shadow of a car hit you. Having no real substance, a shadow is only an appearance. His sheep only walk through the shadow of death. The grave has no hold on a child of God. Certainly, many have closed their eyes in death to this life, but then, no words in the entire vocabulary can describe life on the other side of that shadow.

In great sorrow, His rod and staff shall comfort you. *"As one whom his mother comforts, so I will comfort you;*

and you shall be comforted in Jerusalem." (Isaiah 66:13) In times of sickness, discouragement, or despondency, a warm touch from your Mother's hand is comforting. A word spoken by her may lift your spirit like no other. Nonetheless, the comfort of the Shepherd supersedes the comforting hand or soothing words of a Mother. Sweet consolation, you shall find in the Shepherd.

Wild and vicious animals may be driven away by a rod and staff. Thereby, His rod and staff are used to defend you against the enemy of your soul. Pointing and directing you around the pitfalls set before you, He guides with His rod and staff. A rod also is used as a leaning stick. He is someone to lean upon throughout all of life's journey. By all means, there is great comfort in His rod and staff.

In the presence of your enemies, in the face of all sorts of trials, you are called to the most bountiful table, prepared by the most gracious host. Just imagine you have an open invitation to come and dine at the King's table. In the presence of the Shepherd, your enemies must bow. Never allow the enemy to push you back from the table. An invitation is always open, allowing you to come to the table as often as you desire. The table is never closed.

Families shared a meal together on the night of Passover. A perfect lamb, without a blemish, was served as the main course. Blood from the lamb was sprinkled over each doorpost. Weeping and wailing was heard throughout the night, as the death angel passed through the camp. "Skip over this house," replied the death angel, as it spotted the blood over the doorpost.

The blood of the lamb protected each member of the household from death and delivered them from Egypt. Salvation was found at the table. Jesus Christ represents the table; the blood over the doorpost represents His blood. Salvation and deliverance are still found at the table. As often as you choose, you may come and dine, remembering His loving sacrifice. Offered at the table is sweet communion with the Shepherd. Blessed you are at the table.

Yes, the host at this table is gracious and generous, but all-powerful, as well. By His command, your enemy is rendered powerless. Divine favor of the King of Kings awaits you at the table. Stretched wide across the table is a big banner of love. The choice is yours to make. Accept the invitation to the banquet table or reject His love, protection, deliverance, and salvation. One choice leads to a blessed life, while the other leads to a stressed life.

Despite your enemies, regardless of your heartaches, He will anoint your head. Your cup will overflow. Flies are not only bothersome to humans, but to livestock as well. At certain seasons, flies will attack the sheep, flying around their head, even flying up their nose. If a fly has ever bothered you, then you understand the torment the sheep must endure. Beating their head on the dirt, a post, or by any other means possible, they try to find relief from the troublesome pest. The shepherd of the flock may pour oil over the head of the sheep, in an effort to protect them. The oil drives the flies (the enemy) away. Also, the oil is a healing balm, healing the wounds left behind by the enemy.

The Holy Spirit poured over your head is more refreshing than a cool drink of water on a hot summer day. The oil of the Holy Spirit is a healing agent, healing the hurts and wounds brought on by the enemy. Like a pouring rain that adds life and luster to a dry and parched land, the anointing oil poured over your head revives and restores you to new life. Soaking in the freshness of the Holy Spirit opens your eyes to a new meaning and purpose for your life.

Peace that surpasses all understanding flows from the fountain of the sweet Holy Spirit. As His aroma fills the air, troubled minds are put to rest. Joy floods over your soul, like water overflowing the banks of a mighty river, just by the breath of His holy anointing oil. You shall be empowered by a supernatural strength as He sweeps over you. As the Holy Spirit arises within you, so does your boldness and confidence.

The thief that has come to steal, kill, and destroy you falls powerless as the oil of the Holy Spirit is poured into your life. Stealing the wind out of your sails is Satan's goal. Never fear, the wind beneath your sails is the blowing wind of the Holy Spirit, unleashing a power within you that is mightier than the howling of the enemy. Spilling over into your spirit is a power that is greater than any force that comes against you. *"You are of God, little children, and have overcome them, because He who is in you is greater than he who is in the world."* (1 John 4:4)

You shall lack nothing that is good for you. Good things from the Lord will follow after you all the days of your life. Some of your wants may go lacking, but your needs He will meet. Quite frankly, not all of our wants are always in our best interest. *"For the Lord God is a sun and shield; The Lord will give grace and glory; no good thing will He withhold from those who walk uprightly."* (Psalm 84:11) The sun represents light. He is the light that leads us out of darkness. When in need of guidance, His light will shine upon the path to follow. His shield shall protect us from the darts of the enemy. Blessed we are to have such a wonderful, loving, powerful Shepherd.

Until you lie your head down and breathe your last breath on this earth, His mercy will follow after you. By His Grace, He has prepared a dwelling place for you to abide with Him forever. *"In my Father's house are many mansions; if it were not so, I would have told you. I go to prepare a place for you. And if I go and prepare a place for you, I will come again and receive you to Myself, that where I am, there you may be also."* (John 14:2-3)

There's a good chance that you played a game as a child called "follow the leader." In the child-like game that you would play, a leader would be chosen to follow. After a while, a different person may be chosen as leader. Knowing who the leader was kept you following in line. In real life, there is a leader to follow, who never changes. Jesus Christ, the Good Shepherd, is the leader. He will lead you upon a blessed path that is lined with good things. Follow the leader, and blessings will surely follow you.

CHAPTER 3

Where the Shepherd Leads

Drought in the land was the word that came to Elijah. No rain in sight for three long years. Not exactly the word that you would want to hear concerning your land. No water means no food. Can God bless anyone during a time of drought? Do his blessings stop when the waterspout stops? Of course not. God does not depend upon the rain; He is the maker of the rain. He can and will continue to bless, even in times of a drought. Just ask Elijah.

God instructed Elijah to go eastward over near Jordan to the brook Cherith. According to the command of the Lord, ravens brought food to Elijah at the brook every day. Provision or lack, survival or starvation, which would it be? All hope for Elijah depended upon him following where the Shepherd would lead. His food had been ordered, and delivery instructions had been given to no other place than the brook. Following the Shepherd was of utmost importance. Whatever direction God says to go, there you must go. Just like Elijah, that is your designated place to receive a blessing.

Just as God had promised, each morning Elijah awoke to feast upon bread and meat, which the ravens delivered. In the evenings, wings flapping in the air were like the sound of a dinner bell to Elijah. Looking up into the beautiful sky, seeing the ravens flying in the air was enough to whet his appetite, while he waited for his next meal to arrive. As the days rolled by, he never went hungry. As Elijah was led by the Shepherd, so were the ravens. Even the birds of the air followed where the Shepherd led.

Going westward, away from the direction of the Shepherd, would have proven detrimental for Elijah. Quite frankly, God probably was not going to turn the ravens around with his delicious meal. Water was provided at the brook, and so was his food. Going in the opposite direction would have meant dying of hunger and thirst. Choosing to follow a different path than where the Shepherd leads will surely pull us away from some of our God-assigned blessings.

Elijah had been called to a place of solitude, where he was alone in the presence of God. Some days he may have chosen to sit quietly, meditating on the goodness of the Lord. Soothing his soul, the loving arms of the Shepherd held him in a warm embrace. Other days, Elijah may have stood still or paced the shoreline, giving thanks for all that the Lord had done. All alone at the brook, Elijah may softly utter a prayer, or shout to the top of his lungs. He could weep before the Lord or he could laugh. He could sing a song of praise and clap his hands. The posture of a person or the method of worship does not matter. God sees the heart that is set upon worship. Elijah was led out to the green pasture and down by the still water. During the time of a drought, the Shepherd led him to a place of provision and restoration.

For a season, God took good care of Elijah by the brook, but that season came to an end. Eventually the brook dried up. Now, what was Elijah to do? Would he just sit by the dried up brook until he died? Was that the end of God's provision for him? No, another place was prepared for Elijah. Just because the brook ran dry did not mean that God's blessings had run dry. Again, blessings would be at the end of the trail where the Shepherd led.

Seasons of life come and go for us all. Staying camped out by a stream that has dried up only brings you into a season of drought. By urging you to move along to the next season of life, sometimes, God may mess with your comfort zone. Settled into what is familiar may be most comfortable, but God wants to stretch and move you into new areas of life. Before you can be promoted to your next position, you must be willing to leave your current post of duty. When God has ended one dream, then it is time for a new dream. When He has dried up a stream, then it is time for a new stream. Assuredly, He will lead you to a new place of blessing.

Elijah was told to arise, leave this place of drought. Hmm, could a palace with a bountiful spread on the table be the next stop for Elijah? Most definitely not—God sent him to a place called Zarephath and commanded a widow woman, who was on the verge of starvation herself, to feed him. She had just enough meal and oil to prepare one last meal for herself and her son. In her mind, they would eat, and with nothing left, they would surely die. Rational thinking would not lead anyone who needed food to a poor, destitute widow woman. Elijah had been sitting by a brook without even a crumb on the ground, and he never missed a meal. The ravens never failed to appear with bread and meat as the Lord had instructed them. Therefore, he was not afraid to follow wherever the Shepherd would lead. Instead of rational thinking, Elijah leaned upon the Lord. If the house of the widow woman is where the Lord was leading him, then surely he must go there.

With only a measly amount of oil and meal, her situation certainly seemed mighty bleak. Nonetheless, at the urging of Elijah, she made him a little cake first, gave him a drink of water, and her barrel of meal never ran dry. She followed the instruction of the Lord, as spoken by the prophet Elijah, and she reaped a harvest of blessings as well. Not only did Elijah have plenty to eat, so did the widow woman and her son. When this poor widow woman gave all that she had, God blessed what she had left so greatly that she never ran out. The lady did not simply stretch her skimpy supply of meal and oil to barely make one more cake; the meager amount that seemingly would only serve one more meal lasted for three more years. In the midst of a drought, the Lord provided. Provision came as they each followed the commands of the Lord. Where the Shepherd led, blessings followed.

At the brook, provision came to Elijah by the mouth of the ravens. Then at Zarephath, the hand of a poor widow woman fed him. However, at both places provision came from the same source: the Lord had commanded the blessing. As Elijah walked in obedience to the command of the Lord, he walked into a blessed place. Circumstances did not demand the blessing; God directed Elijah to the place where He had commanded the blessing.

Again, Elijah must follow where the Shepherd would lead. This time he was told to go straight into his enemy's camp. "Go present yourself to Ahab," God said to Elijah. "What? You mean the one who wants to see me dead?" "Yes," God said. Ahab had searched every nation around, looking for Elijah so that he could kill him. His wicked wife, Jezebel, had been responsible for the death of many of God's prophets. "Elijah, you are to go meet your worst enemy face to face." Then God assured Elijah that after his meeting with Ahab, that He would send rain upon the earth. Rain was not coming until Elijah met his stark-raving enemy.

Just as God had been with Elijah at the brook, He was with Him at the widow's house. This time would be no different. He entered the enemy's territory with God on his side. As the Shepherd led Elijah into the land of his enemies, He also protected him. Although Elijah entered into a land where death seemed certain, no harm fell upon him.

Because of the obedience of Elijah, God proved to a nation who had worshipped Baal, a false god, that He was the true God. With a sacrifice placed upon the wood, the prophets of Baal called from morning until noon, asking their false god to strike a fire. They never saw one flicker of a flame. On into the afternoon, they frantically called, weeping, even begging that Baal would cause a fire. All the pleading that they could do, never caused their dead, false god to respond.

But as Elijah began to call upon the Lord God Almighty, fire came down. He even dug a trench, in which he poured buckets of water. In spite of all the water, God still answered by fire. Elijah had told the false prophets that whichever God answered by means of fire, was the true God. Once again, nothing could stop the miracles of God. Then Elijah told Ahab to go and eat; rain was coming to the land.

After three and one half long years, Elijah buried his face between his knees and bowed to the ground, praying earnestly for rain. As Elijah called upon God, an enormous storm began to brew. The winds began to blow, and rain began to pour from the blackened clouds. God heard the prayers of Elijah. *"Elijah was a man with a nature like ours, and he prayed earnestly that it would not rain; and it did not rain on the land for three years and six months. And he prayed again, and the heaven gave rain, and the earth produced its fruit."* (James 5:17-18)

During a time of drought, why would anyone wait for three and a half years to pray for rain? Elijah prayed according to the will of God. Being a faithful and righteous man, he desired God's will above anything else. The rains that came brought much glory and honor unto the Lord. Unbelieving people knew that it was the power of Elijah's God that brought the rain. A continual supply of rain would not have gained their attention like this rain did.

If there is a drought of the Holy Spirit in your life, then no need to wait any longer. Here and now is the time and place to open your heart to receive. Like a pouring rain, He wants to flood your soul with His presence. A touch of the Holy Spirit of God will open your eyes to see things that you have never seen before. A spiritual awakening is on the horizon as you go where He leads.

Unexpected obstacles certainly have a way of popping up along the path of life. Disappointments … we all have had a few. No matter the situation, keep your eyes fastened upon the Shepherd. Elijah could have stayed focused upon the drought, and it would not have brought the rain. Focusing upon your difficulties will not change your situation. Staying focused upon the Shepherd, following where He leads, can take you around troubling issues. Following the Shepherd leads to a blessed life.

CHAPTER 4

My Sheep Know My Voice

How may the Shepherd lead if you do not hear? Elijah followed the Shepherd because he heard and recognized His voice. *"… and the sheep follow Him, for they know His voice."* (John 10:4) The voice of the Shepherd shall lead you and me upon life's journey, as we travel this winding road. His voice is steadfast and sure—a voice that can be trusted like no other. His sheep shall be familiar with His voice.

Beware; He is not the only voice vying for your attention. False voices are ringing out loud and clear. Many voices clamoring in your head at the same time can lead you to a mountain of confusion. "Spin a top and where it lands, there I will go" may seem like an easy alternative. However, you may not like the destination to which the spinning top takes you. False voices do not have a good plan for your life, neither a good path for you to follow.

Follow me, the voice of the Shepherd calls. I will lead you in the path of truth. As you walk in my truth, you shall walk in freedom. *"And you shall know the truth, and the truth shall make you free."* (John 8:32) Shackles will be loosed, and bondages will be broken as you listen to His voice and follow Him. Truth will set you free, while deception will hold you in bondage.

Eve was quite content eating all other fruits of the garden, except the one forbidden fruit, as long as she heeded the voice of God. But then, another voice spoke. Instead of turning a deaf ear to the lie that Satan so cleverly spoke, she listened to his rather interesting sounding voice. Intrigued by the words of Satan, Eve then convinced Adam to listen to him. Following the wrong voice forced them from the beautiful garden that they once called home. Clearly, they had heard the voice of God commanding them to refrain from the forbidden fruit. Now instead of one forbidden fruit, they must leave behind all the delicious fruits that they had enjoyed. Life would never be the same again, all because of listening to one lying voice. God had spoken. Another thought, another voice should never have been entertained.

Not only is Satan a liar, but he invented the lie—the father of lies, he is. Deception is his game plan. On the prowl seeking whom he may deceive. *"Be sober, be vigilant; because your adversary the devil walks about like a roaring lion, seeking whom he may devour."* (1 Peter 5:8) Falling for his lies is as dangerous as falling into the mouth of an angry, roaring lion. Being the sly old fox that he is, he will eat away at you with one little lie after another. A nibble here and a nibble there until he has completely devoured you. His aim is to turn your God ordained blessings into his evil curses.

Portraying evil as good and good as evil is no new trick to the devil. If we all saw evil for what it is, there would be no temptation. Everyone else is doing it, so it must be good. That is a line that he has used for centuries. He is certain to point out the good times everyone else seems to be enjoying. But never does he show the big steel chain that he has waiting to wrap around them, holding them in deep bondage. Recognizing his deceitful voice will have you running the other way. Not only is it important to know the voice of the Shepherd, it is equally imperative to know when it is the voice of another.

Recognizing voices, separating truth from what is false is vitally important. The Shepherd most often speaks through His written word. Although He does speak through a still small voice, He will never speak anything contrary to the Holy Scriptures. Allow the Holy Bible to be the measuring instrument, deciphering truth or not. Knowing truth allows you to recognize the false.

Mirror, mirror on the wall, shine your reflection upon my heart. A mirror is a reflection of what is real. The reason we stand in front of a mirror styling our hair, putting on makeup, adjusting clothing before leaving home, is because that mirror reveals truth, the way we really look. The Word of God is like that mirror, revealing truth. What is in line with His word, and what stands against His word, can only be observed through His word. Satan's lies cannot hide in the mirror of truth. Of course, that mirror probably is not hanging on your wall. Maybe it lies upon your coffee table, nightstand, or possibly tucked away in a closet somewhere. Now is the time to open up the pages, read and study His Word, and see the reflection of Christ. Through the pages, you shall hear and know His voice. Through the voice of the Shepherd, the lies of the enemy are highlighted, helping you to know the difference.

Hold a mirror up before your eyes in the dark, and you will see nothing. An image can only be revealed in a mirror as rays of light are reflected on the mirror surface. Jesus Christ is the light that is reflected in His Word, revealing truth. *"I am the light of the world. He who follows me shall not walk in darkness, but have the light of life."* (John 8:12) Darkness snuffs out the light, leaving one to grope along in the darkness. However, light dispels the darkness, lighting your pathway. Jesus Christ, the light of the world, exposes the lies of the enemy. You will either live in the darkness of this world, or the light of Jesus Christ. Hearing and knowing His voice will be the determining factor in choosing light or darkness, truth or deception.

While words of wisdom to live by are found in His word, He also speaks into our heart with His still small voice. However, entertaining every thought that pops into your head as a word spoken by the Lord can be dangerous. Some of our own self-imposed thoughts can be quite entertaining. Let's not forget that the sly old fox, Satan, also comes along trying to weave his ideas into your imagination. If a thought does not align itself with the written word, then you can be certain that is not a God thought. Remember, knowing truth helps you to recognize the false. The sheep shall know His voice, but also recognize the voice of the enemy.

When wrestling with thoughts and ideas in my own personal life, not knowing what I should or shouldn't do with a matter, or what steps I should take, another person has often spoken clarity to me. Sitting in church on a Sunday morning, pondering on a thought that had come to me during the week, seeking an answer, many times the confirmation would come through a word that the pastor spoke. The pastor was completely unaware of the answers that I was seeking. This was a God word, planted into the heart of another person, speaking wisdom unto me. The voice of God had spoken; I needed to listen.

A number of years ago, I walked into my weekly Sunday school class as I did any other normal Sunday. Taking my seat, the teacher stepped up in front of the class as usual. This particular day, my ordinary Sunday morning turned into anything but ordinary. As the teacher began to speak, an overwhelming urgency flooded up within me. Over and over in my soul I could hear the words, "you need to be teaching a Sunday school class." I literally wanted to get up, leave the class, and find a class to teach. That same Sunday morning, as usual, I left Sunday school class and walked into the sanctuary for morning service. As any other normal Sunday would be, I was handed a bulletin upon entering the church. As I opened the bulletin, I saw big, bold letters that read, "We desperately need Sunday school teachers." I instantly knew that I was supposed to be one of them. That morning I heard the voice of the Shepherd calling deep within my spirit. Quickly, I received a word through the bulletin, confirming what I had heard. He had spoken; my responsibility was to hear and obey.

God is not limited on how to speak. Regardless of the method wherein we hear His voice, it demands our attention. A few years ago, someone who is very dear to me was struggling with a decision that needed to be made. Praying, seeking, and listening for God to speak, she drove past a church. Standing tall on the church marquee the answer was right in front of her eyes. The verse that they had put on the church sign may have been especially placed there for her. It was the voice of the Shepherd giving her divine direction.

Sweet words of consolation oftentimes are whispered in the ear of one who is struggling along the way. Some voices might say you are too frail, too small, and too weak; you shall never make it. But the voice of the Shepherd says, you are made strong through My strength; My sufficiency swallows up your insufficiency. Discouragement must flee at the sound of His command. When His voice speaks, stand still and listen. Soon His voice will drown out the chatter of the false voices.

An intimate relationship with the Shepherd grabs our attention to listen for His voice. That same intimacy tunes our ears to hear. Eager to hear the Shepherd speak, Mary attentively sat at His feet. Her sister, Martha, was in quite a stew, thinking how unfair for Mary to just be sitting while she was busy with all the work. Avoiding household chores, forcing Martha to pick up the slack, was not Mary's intent. Instead Mary simply chose to sit quietly in the presence of her Lord and soak in His every word. He had something to speak, and she wanted to hear. Devoting her time to Him and lending her ear to His word was of greater importance than anything else. Jesus commended Mary because she had chosen the better thing. Her undivided attention was a worship unto the Lord. Obviously, chores do need to be done. Jesus was not forbidding work; instead, He emphasized that worship is the greater thing.

Intimacy with Him tunes your ear to hear His voice—the voice that has no boundaries. You cannot run far enough away that you cannot hear Him speak. Jonah heard His voice while floating in the belly of a fish. Paul heard His voice while traveling down a road on his way to persecute believers. Hearing His voice prompted a change of direction in each of their lives. His voice shall always point us in the right direction. All those who are His sheep shall know and recognize His voice.

CHAPTER 5

Blessed by Obedience

His sheep shall hear His voice and know His voice; then, they shall obey His voice. Vain and empty words have never been uttered out of His mouth. Each word that He speaks is spoken with divine authority for a divine purpose, and ultimately for our good. Therefore, listening intently and obeying what we hear will serve us well. Hearing the word is one thing; obedience is another. Your blessing is found in obedience. *"Blessed are those who hear the word of God and keep it."* (Luke 11:28) God did not create a list of rules to be harsh, nor hard to follow. Taking all the fun out of life was never His intent. His commands are for the good of mankind. Obedience is a stepping-stone, leading to your blessed life.

Blessed by obedience was the song of the day for one wedding party. All the guests had arrived for the blissful occasion. Celebration was in full swing as the wedding festivities were well underway. Suddenly, all the wine bottles were empty. Disastrous, the host thought. They did not realize that a certain special guest, who was in attendance, was the solution. They did not understand the blessing of having Jesus in the house.

Mary said to Jesus, her son, *"They have no wine."* (John 2:3) Jesus warned His Mother that the time had not yet come for His identity or powers to be revealed. Nevertheless, she advised the host, *"Whatsoever He says to you, do it."* (John 2:5) Wow, what a concept! Just do whatever He says—a powerful statement, but oh so true. Blessings come by simply doing whatever He says.

Jesus responded by saying, *"Fill the water pots with water."* (John 2:7) Six water pots filled with water were set before Him. Amazingly, normal water was turned into an extraordinary tasting wine. The finest of wines was presented to the host. He questioned, "Why have we waited until now to serve this choice wine?" Doing whatever He said came alive to those who witnessed such a miracle. His word became real because they did as He said. Somewhere in between the command and the fabulous wine was an act of obedience.

Of course, Jesus could have splashed wine into the empty bottles. He did not need their help; neither did He even need water. He wanted their obedience. On that day, a lesson of obedience was surely learned. Just do as He says do is still good advice to follow. Blessings flow out of obedience.

Just do as He says paid off big for Peter and a few other disciples. A long night of fishing netted them not one fish. But everything changed when Jesus came by. Jesus commanded Peter to cast his net on the right side of the boat, out into the deep water. *"But Simon (Peter) answered and said to Him, Master, we have toiled all night and caught nothing; nevertheless at your word I will let down the net."* (Luke 5:5) Peter let his net down one more time because Jesus had said so. As he obeyed the command of the Lord, the fish that had dodged him all night entered into the net. This was no normal catch of fish. Toiling and tugging, they landed a haul of fish that was heavy enough to break their nets. Obedience commanded the fish to enter into the net. In between the command of the Lord and the blessed catch of fish was Peter's obedience.

Fishing all night had filled the boat with nothing but disappointment, but they would not allow discouragement to rob them of their blessing. Peter instantly replied, "although we have cast all night, and caught nothing, at your word, Lord, we will cast again." Many people would have said after fishing all this time, there is no use to cast another time. Peter's obedience was not founded on his current situation, which was an empty fishing net. Neither was it based on human reasoning. His obedience was solely centered on the Word of the Lord. Continue obeying the Lord, even when you don't see the results that you were expecting. Simply do whatever He says to do.

Obedience sometimes comes with resistance, as was the case with Naaman, who desperately needed a miracle. A terrible case of leprosy racked his entire body. Painful sores, which were disgusting looking, covered him from head to toe. Society looked upon him as a shame and disgrace. Naaman would have been willing to do anything the medical staff suggested. He would have paid any amount of money to have his skin made well. But, following the command of the Lord to dip himself seven times in the Jordan River seemed completely absurd to him. Yet that was exactly the command of the Lord.

The very thought of dipping down into the Jordan River sent Naaman into a fit of rage. After all, other rivers have much cleaner water. How could the dirty water of the Jordan River heal his leprosy? Dipping into the Jordan River simply made no sense to Naaman. Human logic turned him from heeding the command that would ultimately lead to his healing.

At the urging of his servants, he reluctantly went to the Jordan River. Thank God for those persistent servants who finally convinced Naaman to obey. Dipping himself down one time was not enough. After six times, leprosy still covered his body. But, the seventh time coming up out of that water wrote another story. Another miracle has been performed! Meticulously examining his body, Naaman found nothing but pure, clean skin. As he followed the command of the Lord, his skin had been made as fresh as that of a little child. Obedience was the stepping-stone between God's command and the healed skin.

God could have miraculously healed Naaman without him going into the Jordan River or any other river, for that matter. But his healing demanded obedience. Naaman's world was changed as he obeyed the instruction of the Lord. Stepping out of his box with his own preconceived ideas was in order for Naaman. Healing did not come in the way that Naaman was expecting. Surely, Elisha would come with healing in his hands,

Naaman supposed. Healed by way of obedience to the Lord opened his eyes to the glory of God, the ultimate healer. Otherwise, he would have given honor to Elisha. He also knew that he had done nothing to earn his healing. Naaman experienced the transforming power of God on a deeper level than just having his body healed.

Many of life's blessings hinge on a doorway called obedience. The same hinge that opens a door will also close the same door. Obedience can be like that open door, allowing blessings to flow through. Obeying the Lord opens your hand to receive. Disobedience may become a closed fist that turns away the blessings that lie in wait for you. If Satan can steal your obedience, then he can steal your victory.

The blessed Promised Land laid just ahead of the Israelites. A victory march was just a few short days away, but disobedience robbed them of their victory lap. Sadly, they wandered around their blessing for forty years, yet they never received their promise. Only two obedient soldiers, Joshua and Caleb, entered the land. God was not slack granting His promise. By way of disobedience, the Israelites simply failed to receive. The next generation marched into the Promise Land, receiving the blessing that their forefathers rejected.

Obedience is not a fast track around disappointments. Challenges, hardships, and pain come to us all. Jesus even warned us of these things. *"In the world ye shall have tribulation: but be of good cheer; I have overcome the world."* (John 16:33) He, who has a life of purpose planned for you, has overcome the trials that you face.

Jumping off of the obedience track will surely derail you from some of your greatest blessings.

Obedience does not mean that you walk step by step perfectly. The only one who ever lived a perfect life shed His innocent blood upon the cross, died and rose again, to cover our mistakes. Through His blood, every stain of our sins has been made clean. By His Grace, we stand before Him just as if we never sinned. By His Grace, I am blessed. If you are expecting perfection then look to Jesus; all others fall way short of the mark.

Rest assuredly; He has a good plan for you and me. Obedience does not mean that there will be no hurdles to jump. Obedience propels you to jump the hurdle, instead of standing grumbling at the obstacle. Blessings may be on the other side of a tall mountain that you must climb, or a river that you must swim. Allow God to swoop you up into His arms and be your mountain climber. Stroke for stroke, swim in stride with Him. Disobedience is like swimming against the tide—the undercurrent pulling you farther out to sea, farther away from your greatest blessings.

Obedience surrenders our will to His will. Coming into agreement with Him, we partner with Him in what He is doing. Disobedience works against Him; it also works against our own good. He has prepared a greater good for us than we can fathom. Not only does He have our good at heart, He also has the foresight to know what is best for us, and the power and authority to bring it to pass. Many blessings lie within the boundaries of His Word.

CHAPTER 6
Commitment

Settle in your mind to follow the Lord. Obedience will never happen without a commitment. Leading you down a road of failure and one disappointment after another would be a commitment based on rules and regulations. A long list of do's and don'ts is very demanding and extremely tiring. You have entered into a deeper realm of satisfaction when you enter into a commitment based on a relationship. Loving Jesus is fulfilling and greatly rewarding. As your intimacy with Christ grows deeper, so does your commitment. Love is the foundation on which commitment is founded.

Adorned in an elegant wedding gown with a gorgeous long train flowing behind, a beaming bride looks absolutely stunning as she gracefully walks down the aisle. With her face all aglow, sparkling eyes, and bright smile, guests can sense love in the atmosphere. Anxiously awaiting the arrival of his lovely bride, her handsome bridegroom stands in awe of her beauty. Dressed in a well-fitting tuxedo, he stands with his heart about to beat out of his chest with pride. Standing hand in hand, they exchange wedding vows, proclaiming their love one for another. Before family, friends, and God, they make a life-long commitment to each other. From this moment forward, happy ever after shall be their song. At least that is the plan.

Sometimes, the happy ever after falls apart. The day comes, when those same eyes that beamed with joy are glaring at each other with anger. The same heart that once beat with pride now pounds with madness. All the big, bright smiles are turned into sad frowns. Strolling hand in hand no longer exist. Commitment becomes a distant memory. In the process of broken promises, hearts are broken.

Long before you were formed in your mother's womb, a bridegroom stood by waiting to receive you as His bride. Instead of a fancy tuxedo, He chose a robe and a crown of thorns as His wedding garment. Ink from some fine ink well did not scribble your wedding vows on some fancy scroll. His vows of commitment were written with every drop of His red blood. His commitment of love was not sealed in a huge, magnificent cathedral with a pipe organ and festivities. His commitment of love was signed, sealed, and delivered upon a hillside of Golgotha as an angry mob stood by, shouting out "crucify Him." Forever, He will remain true to His love and commitment to you. Blessed you are to be called His bride.

The very voice that spoke the world into existence could have spoken the nails to come out of His hands and feet. If He had spoken the word, nails would have gone flying through the air. Nails did not have the power to hold Him on the cross. Instead, love was the driving force that held Him there. He could have called thousands of angels to His rescue. Angel wings flapping through the air would have been heard for miles around, had He so chosen. The same love that nailed Him to the cross held Him on the cross. He willingly died so that you and I could live eternally with Him. No greater commitment could ever be made. No greater blessing could ever be found than the blessing of the cross. *"Greater love has no one than this, than to lay down one's life for his friends."* (John 15:13) Blessed are those who are called His friend.

He has clothed you in a beautiful wedding garment, called the righteousness of Christ. Attached to your wedding apparel is a long list of blessings, benefits beyond your wildest imaginations. Commitment is included in these wedding vows as well. *"If you love me, keep my commandments."* (John 14:15) Be assured of this one thing—that Christ, your bridegroom, will always remain true to His commitment. He will never fail you. *"I will never leave you nor forsake you."* (Hebrews 13:5) But just as surely as we breathe air into our lungs, in our human nature, we will fail from time to time. In your times of failure, your heavenly Father will hold your hand, helping you to find your way again. Child, get up, brush yourself off, and continue on your journey, committed to your heavenly Father. Yes, you have also been blessed to be called His child.

Submission flows out of love. Commitment will never happen without submission. An act of submission to the Father led Jesus to the cross. Great sorrow gripped His heart while in the garden of Gethsemane.

In anguish, Jesus prayed, asking if possible that this cup could pass from Him. But was sure to end His prayer with a willingness to drink of the cup if that was the will of the Father. *"He went a little farther and fell on His face, and prayed, saying, 'O My Father, if it is possible, let this cup pass from Me: nevertheless, not as I will, but as You will."* (Matthew 26:39) Jesus was not referring to the cruel death that He was about to experience. Bearing the sins of all the world was the heaviness that grieved His spirit. Since there was no other way, He gladly would take on the sins of the world, endure the agony of the cross, and shed His blood to pay the penalty of the sins of mankind. Because of love, He was submissive. Blessed we are because He was submissive to the Father.

Relinquishing your own desires to another is submission. Too many to count are the blessings heading your way as you surrender your own agenda, plans, and ideas to Christ. Demanding your own way just may have you side-stepping many of those blessings designed especially for you. *"Therefore submit to God. Resist the devil and he will flee from you."* (James 4:7) Our own strength would fail us in our feeble attempts to resist the devil without first being submissive to God. Submission to God is a powerful weapon against the evil one who is out to steal the abundant life that Christ came to give. Blessed you will be in your submission.

Submission comes from a humble spirit. Christ was born as the King of Kings and the Lord of Lords. He is the highest form of royalty. Yet humbly, He was born in a stable, wrapped in swaddling clothes, and laid in a manger. He humbled Himself enough to die upon the cross for all of the world. *"And being found in appearance as a man, He humbled Himself and became obedient to the point of death, even the death of the cross. Therefore God also has highly exalted Him and given Him the name which is above every name, that at the name of Jesus every knee should bow, of those in heaven, and of those on earth, and of those under the earth, and that every tongue should confess that Jesus Christ is Lord, to the glory of God the Father."* (Philippians 2:8-11) In a spirit of humility, Christ was submissive, and became obedient, even to death. Then, He was exalted. Humbly, He placed the needs of mankind before His own comfort. Christ is the ultimate example of humility.

Humbleness is not weakness. Understanding where your strength comes from is humility. We can only be strong through the strength of the Lord. His mighty power working in each of us can accomplish the mission that He has set for us. My own strength and power can do nothing. Humbleness realizes that the enabling and equipping of skills and abilities come by His Grace.

Only through a spirit of humbleness, will anyone recognize that they need Christ. No one will come to the Savior, unless they understand they need a Savior. All who have surrendered to Christ, submitted themselves unto Him and committed to His ways, have humbly realized that His ways are better than their own. No matter what position in life you hold, always remain humble. Remember, the same God that elevated you can also bring you down. Blessings are sure to follow the humble in spirit.

On the other hand, arrogance is self-serving. Demeaning others, feeling superior over them, is an arrogance that is a stink in the nostrils of God. *"For I say, through the grace given to me, to everyone who is among you, not to think of himself more highly than he ought to think, but to think soberly, as God has dealt to each one a measure of faith."* (Romans 12:3) God is the maker of us all. He did not create one to be more special than the other. Finding gratification in humiliating a fellow human is prideful. Pride will never find a way to submit. *"God resists the proud, But gives grace to the humble."* (James 4:6) Pride is a spirit that He will reject, while humbleness is accepted and blessed.

Commitment must be consistent. Commitment was the lifestyle of Daniel. Consistently, Daniel knelt on his knees and prayed unto God three times daily. The king, being persuaded by evil men, signed a decree forbidding anyone to pray for thirty days. Being thrown into a den of lions would be the punishment for breaking the decree. As Daniel always did, he continued bowing down on his knees in front of his window, praying to God. Just as the decree had stated, Daniel was cast into the den of lions.

The king was distraught because he loved Daniel and did not want him harmed. "Daniel, your God will deliver you," the king confidently declared. Sure enough, angels were dispersed by God's command and shut the mouths of the lions. All night long, Daniel sat in a den of lions, and not one lion took a bite of him.

Faced with the threat of being cast into a den of hungry lions, Daniel remained consistent to his commitment. He was blessed with divine protection.

Commitment offers no room for compromise. The Word of God is the foundation of our faith. In spite of all else, stand firm upon the Word. God's principles are not to be compromised. Do not be swayed by popular opinions that are opposed to the will of God. Swaying between two belief systems is unstable. *"... he is a double-minded man, unstable in all his ways."* (James 1:8) Those who profess Christianity must stand for His truth, without compromise. When commitment gives way to compromise, then commitment no longer exists. Some of life's blessings will surely be forfeited in the world of compromise.

Summoned upon Mount Sinai, Moses left his brother, Aaron, in charge of the Israelites. Increasingly, they became impatient as Moses lingered upon the mountain. "Make us gods," they said to Aaron. Without hesitation, Aaron says, "Take off your golden earrings." Using the gold, Aaron shaped and molded a golden calf for them to worship. Aaron, of all people, the high priest, should have known better. He built an altar declaring a feast day as a day unto the Lord. They even honored pieces of gold that they had soldered together, as the gods who brought them out of Egypt. They compromised because they did not see what they were looking for, which was Moses coming down from the mountain.

How committed were they? Seems that they had their eyes fixed upon Moses instead of looking to

God. Moses was the object of their faith. When the object of their faith went missing, they went searching for another. Then, the golden calf, a worthless image that could be broken, became the substance of their faith. Worship to anything or anyone else other than God is worship to a false idol. *"You shall have no other gods before me."* (Exodus 20:3) Commitment to God becomes compromised when we look to another source. When commitment becomes compromised, then commitment ceases.

A committed life to Jesus Christ begins with love, and submits to His authority through the spirit of humility. Commitment remains consistent, refusing to compromise. Commitment will stand firm in the face of some of life's most challenging moments. That same commitment will keep you standing firm, as well. Obedience may be the stepping-stone to blessings. But commitment is the cement that holds the stones in place. A life committed to Christ is a blessed life.

CHAPTER 7

In the Shepherd I Will Trust

Add fuel to a fire and watch the flames shoot high into the sky. The flickering flame setting a spark to your commitment is trust. Your commitment may be measured by the level of your submission, which is determined by the depth of your trust. No one will ever submit to what they cannot trust. Love is the burning torch that ignites the flame of trust. Love, trust, submission, and commitment fuel one another. Your commitment will never burn out as long as you keep the flames of love and trust burning.

His love for you and me soars higher than the heavens, spreads wider than the big blue sky, and runs deeper that the ocean floor. His love, which is not based on your looks, performance, or behavior, is the purest of all loves. He loves without end. His everlasting love went all the way to the cross. *"But God demonstrates His own love toward us, in that while we were still sinners, Christ died for us."* (Romans 5:8) The human mind cannot understand such intimacy. Love is not just an action that Christ does. Rather, love is His true nature. The characteristic that defines Him is Love—unquestionable, His love can be trusted.

Trusting the Shepherd is birthed out of intimacy with Him. Keeping Jesus tucked away in a forsaken corner somewhere, only to pull Him out when troubles come your way, will never develop into an intimate relationship. Like all other loving relationships, intimacy grows by spending time together. Abiding in His presence makes the heart grow fonder. Fall completely in love with Him, and trust will follow.

More than a cliché, the words "In God we trust" shall be our standard of life. Trusting the Lord with all your heart is a firm foundation on which to stand. You shall not lose your footing; you shall neither stumble nor fall as long as your heart remains fixed upon trusting Him. Without trust, the ground will surely shake and crumble under your feet. *"Blessed is the man who trust in The Lord, and whose hope is in the Lord."* (Jeremiah 17:7) Clinging to hope in any other source is a false hope.

He is our only secure hope. He is the only firm foundation on which to stand. He is the only One that you can depend upon all the days of your life. All others may become overpowered or overruled. Kings rise and fall, but the authority of God shall stand forever. His authority can be trusted. Remember, it was He who came to give you an abundantly blessed life. Also, understand that He is the only one who has the power and authority to grant such a promise. His authority never ends.

Strong as an ox, you may say. All the might and strength of a yoke of oxen will one day fail. Your own strength will also fade away. The power and might of the Shepherd is greater than the strength of a team of wild horses. His strength shall never weaken, nor fade. Neither shall His authority ever be overruled. Forever, you may rely upon His power and authority.

Believing that the Shepherd will carry out my own plans to my own specifications is far from trusting Him. Being confident in His will for my life is trust. As we pray the beautiful rendition of the Lord's prayer, we pray, *"Your kingdom come. Your will be done on earth as it is in heaven."* (Matthew 6:10) By means of submission, we ask that His rule and reign take precedence in our request. We shall always trust the Father to bring His will to pass, rather than our own, praying, "Lord, here is my petition. Please do with it as You will." Instead of trusting that your every little wish will be granted, believe that He will carry out His best for you.

Surrendering our will to the Good Shepherd is an act of trust. As the Shepherd tenderly and lovingly leads the sheep, trust keeps the sheep walking in line with Him. You may cast all your cares upon Him as you trust in His care. Trust depends upon His ways instead of demanding our own way. His ways are always much higher than our own. *"For my thoughts are not your thoughts, nor are your ways My ways, says the Lord. For as the heavens are higher than the earth, so are My ways higher than your ways, and My thoughts than your thoughts."* (Isaiah 55:8–9) Trusting Him will have you scaling heights much higher than your own plans.

Trust will say, "God, I want all that You have intended for me and absolutely nothing that You do not want for me." He knows what is for my good and what is meant for my harm.

Lean upon His wisdom and not your own. *"Trust in the Lord with all your heart, and lean not on your own understanding. In all your ways acknowledge Him, and He shall direct your paths."* (Proverbs 3:5-6) He is the only One who is worthy of complete trust. Leaning upon anything other than Him is like leaning upon a broken brick wall. Though, it may look sturdy, your weight upon the old broken wall will surely cause it to fall. Leaning upon Him recognizes that you are totally dependent upon Him. Therefore, you do not rely upon your own strength, abilities, or wisdom. Rather, understanding that your own strength is very weak, abilities extremely limited, and human wisdom is very lacking, therefore, lean upon the One who knows all things and has no limitations. Standing fully confident in Him, allowing Him full charge of your life is Trust!

His Word can be trusted. Never has there ever been a more reliable word, spoken or written, than the Word of God. *"And the Word became flesh and dwelt among us, and we beheld His glory, the glory as of the only begotten of the Father, full of grace and truth."* (John 1:14) He is the word, which became flesh. Doubting His word is to doubt Him. However, faith in His word is faith in Him.

Unequivocally, you may place all of your trust in His Word, because He is always faithful to keep His Word. *"For all the promises of God in Him are Yes, and in*

Him Amen, to the glory of God through us." (2 Corinthians 1:20) His Word is completely reliable and trustworthy. He never changes his mind. Therefore, His Word never changes. *"Forever, O Lord, your word is settled in heaven."* (Psalm 119:89) If you could measure forever in days, months, or years, then you could determine a date that His Word becomes null and void. But forever never ends, and neither do the truth, power, and authority of His Word.

Blessed are those who heed the Word of the Lord, rather than taking counsel from the ungodly. *"Blessed is the man who walks not in the counsel of the ungodly, nor stands in the path of sinners, nor sits in the seat of the scornful; But his delight is in the law of the Lord, and in His law he meditates day and night."* (Psalm 1:1-2) This is a pronounced blessing over those who will walk according to the ways of the Lord, instead of opposed to Him. How shall we know the ways of the Lord? By His Word! Living by His Word makes for a blessed life.

Trusting His Word leads to obeying His Word. On the other hand, a lack of trust will lead to rebellion. One's own opinion of His Word will never substitute for the real thing. We can know Him through His Word, not by opinions and assumptions. His Word is truth; therefore we shall rely upon the Holy Scriptures as they are written. *"So then faith comes by hearing, and hearing by the word of God."* (Romans 10:17) Unless you believe the Truth, you will be led by deception. Truth leads to the abundant life that Christ came to give, while deception leads to a cursed life.

Trusting more makes for worrying less! Worry makes your fears come alive. Frayed nerves are settled by trusting the Shepherd. Fears are tamed, as you trust in the Lord. *"Whenever I am afraid, I will trust in You."* (Psalm 56:3) Like all other humans, David faced fears. Most of us have never faced the same kind of fear that David faced, such as being chased by an enemy with murder in his heart. But David's response to fear was to trust in the Lord. David also understood that the Lord was his shepherd, who would guide him through every rough terrain that he encountered. Therefore, he could place his trust in Him and Him alone.

David knew what it was to trust in the Lord in times of great distress. In one of those troublesome times David rejoiced in The Lord. *"But I have trusted in Your mercy; my heart shall rejoice in Your salvation."* (Psalm 13:5) When we find ourselves standing in troubled waters, we can rejoice to the God of our salvation, because we know our help comes from the Lord. We, too, shall trust and not be afraid.

Fearful events happen in all of our lives. However, we do not need to be tormented with fear. Like shackles tied around your ankles, fear stops you in your tracks. No need to stand with feet bound. Trust loosens the shackles, setting you free. Trust allows you to walk through fearful times in peace instead of torment. By trusting the Shepherd, a dreaded occurrence can be met with a peaceful mindset.

The three Hebrew children trusted in the Lord, their God, as they were thrown into a red-hot fiery furnace. Though King Nebuchadnezzar had decreed that all would bow and worship the golden image that he had made, Shadrach, Meshach, and Abednego refused. Heat up the furnace seven times hotter was the command of the King. Bind them up and cast them in the fire, King Nebuchadnezzar demanded. Knowing the penalty, these three steadfastly stood in allegiance to the Lord. Their commitment to Him did not waver because their trust did not waver.

Burned alive by the hot flames of the fire was the fate of the men who threw them into the furnace. But not a hair on any of the three Hebrew children was singed. No harm was done to these faithful men, who trusted the Lord. "We threw three men into the fire, but I see four," exclaimed King Nebuchadnezzar! In total amazement, the King announced, "The fourth man looks like the son of God." Looks were not deceiving on that day. The Son of God truly was walking around in the fire, protecting His children. He is your lifeline, just as He was to these three fine young men.

Things cannot be trusted because the day will come that they will fail. People may have good intentions, but many limitations. Hindrances are certain to prevent your friends and family from coming to your rescue. But the name of the Lord can be trusted at all times and through all situations. *"Some trust in chariots, and some in horses; but we will remember the name of the Lord our God."* (Psalm 20:7) His name has no boundaries that it cannot cross, neither hindrances that it cannot push through.

He is a strong defense to all who trust in Him. *"The Lord is good, a stronghold in the day of trouble; and He knows those who trust in Him."* (Nahum 1:7) His name is powerful and mighty enough to be worthy of your trust. *"The name of the Lord is a strong tower; the righteous run into it and are safe."* (Proverbs 18:10) Calling upon His name in complete confidence is your strong defense. Readily available to you at all times is a strong tower where you will be safe from the enemy. Strap on your running shoes and run into the tower, called the name of the Lord. These shoes were not made in some elaborate manufacturing plant nor stamped with an expensive name brand on them. Trust in His name made those shoes. You may wear the shoes of trust at all times and any occasion.

Since He cares for the birds of the air, the fishes in the sea, and the cattle upon the earth, then surely, He cares for you and me. If He cares enough about you to count each hair upon your head, then certainly He cares about every detail of your life. He has you wrapped tighter in His arms than a loving mother would wrap around her newborn baby. He is your strong defender against all evil that comes against you. He is the source of all that you need. He is the one of whom you may boldly say *"The Lord is my helper; I will not fear. What can man do to me?"* (Hebrews 13:6) He is the Good Shepherd. He cares for you! Place your trust in Him!

CHAPTER 8

Blessings From the Pit

A blessed life that takes you from here into eternity is the Shepherd's plan. However, Satan's plan is to drag you into a pit of gloom and hopelessness. If only he could, he would wrap a chain around you, dragging you all the way down to the very bottom of the pit—laughing all the way, of course. But his plans unravel as the Good Shepherd arises in your defense. He can still be trusted even when it seems that you are in a pit of despair. The Shepherd renders the pit powerless.

We probably all have danced around the pit a few times. Maybe occasionally we dangled over the edge. Most of us may have had a few days that we almost drown ourselves in a pit. A feeling of helplessness settled in, as it seemed that we would buckle underneath a heavy load. But we must remember that He does not weigh us down with more than we can carry. Not wanting His sheep to bear a heavy burden, He came to lift that heaviness off of you. Release that heavy load unto Him, then He will put a new song in your heart, a new spring in your step, and renew your hope. He will carry you far away from the pit.

Senseless thoughts swirling round and round in your head are certain to lead you straight to a pit of confusion. How did I get here? What do I do now? Where do I go? How can I possibly get out of this mess? Perhaps these are some of the questions flooding your mind. Seems that your mind jumped on a merry-go-round with no off switch. But, faith in Jesus Christ is the off switch to confusion and the on switch to sanity. Christ is not the author of confusion. Turmoil was created by the devil himself; Christ is the author of peace. *"For God is not the author of confusion but of peace."* (1 Corinthians 14:33) He is the answer to all your questions. Knowing how to fix your mess is not nearly as important as knowing who can fix your mess. Knowing who can lead you out of the pit is much better than trying to find your own way out—or worse yet, curling up in a ball to stay in the pit. Jesus is the only place to turn.

Hope founded upon circumstances will certainly have you crawling into a pit. Life is ever changing. Thrills and excitement may overwhelm you today, only to have discouragement and disappointments drag you into the pit tomorrow. Out of the pit you come, trying to make sense of life's ups and downs. Just when the wheels of life begin running smoothly again, suddenly, another wheel comes loose, bouncing off in an unexpected direction. That is the cycle of life. But Jesus Christ remains steady and sure. He is an ever constant, never changing God. *"Jesus Christ is the same yesterday, today, and forever."* (Hebrews 13:8) Do not become disheartened when the unexpected and unwelcomed twists and turns of life come your way. God still loves you and is still working all things out for your good. Come out of the pit, lift up your head, for you are blessed.

My, how life took a sudden turn for Joseph! Being the favorite child of his dad may have granted him specials perks with Daddy, but certainly not with his brothers. In his father's eyes, Joseph was a cut above all the rest of his children. Gazing upon Joseph brought a little brighter sparkle to Dad's eyes than his other children. Stirring the flames of jealousy, Joseph strutted about in a gorgeous coat that Dad made especially for him. This coat, made with rich, vibrant colors, spoke of Dad's love for Joseph. But to his brothers, this beautiful garment was a symbol of Dad's favoritism. Even the sight of this coat made his brothers hot with anger. They fumed with jealousy until they were green with envy. Anger and jealousy are a bad combination, and this case was no different.

Stoking the flames of jealousy even hotter, Joseph proudly shared his dreams, which showed Joseph would become superior over his brothers. Maybe an older, more mature brother would have kept his dreams to himself. Nevertheless, young Joseph seemed quite pleased to announce that his dreams revealed his family bowing down and serving him. Who does he think that he is? What makes him think that we should bow to him, they questioned. Soon their jealousy turned into bitterness. It didn't take long until hate filled their heart. They despised their own brother.

One day as his brothers were out tending to the flock, his father sent Joseph to check on them. Of course, Dad did not realize that he was sending his prized son into great danger. The very sight of Joseph infuriated his brothers. Each step that he took toward them, their fierce anger fumed a little hotter. They were boiling mad by the time that Joseph reached them. As Joseph approached his despiteful brothers, anger, jealousy, and hate spewed out of them like the eruption of a hot volcano.

Quickly, they devised an evil plot to take Joseph out for good. Ending his life would surely be the end of his dreams. Kill the dreamer boy and throw him into a pit. That will be the end of him and his dreams, they thought. Sparing his life, his oldest brother, Ruben, came to his rescue. Pleading with the other brothers, Ruben urged them not to kill Joseph. Throw him into the pit alive, Ruben suggested. So into the pit Joseph went. Ruben actually had a plan to come back later and deliver his brother from the pit.

Little did Ruben know that his plan to deliver his brother would be greatly interrupted? Before he could deliver Joseph out of the pit, a band of men headed for Egypt came by. In a blink of an eye, Joseph was sold as a slave and headed for Egypt. Good riddance, surmised his brothers. Out of sight for good, we will never see him again, they supposed.

Ruben's plan failed because God had a better plan. God had a greater deliverance in mind than pulling Joseph out of the pit. Satan came to cast him down. But God intended to raise him up. Joseph was cast deep into a pit, then walked a long, hard road to Egypt, yet God never took His hand off of him. His mean, old hateful brothers could steal his beautiful, cherished coat, cast him into a deep, dark pit, and even sell him into another land. But they could not steal the blessings of God.

Joseph could have wallowed in a pit of self-pity. After all, being the pampered one, he was accustomed to the good life. Away from home, he was away from all that was familiar to him. Even dear, reliable Dad could not come to his rescue this time. "Woe unto me" would have been the song that many would have been singing. Self-pity is a pit of mud that blinds the eyes so severely that a person can see no good thing coming their way. Self-pity fails to see the blessings of God.

A pit of worry could have been his fate. Curled up in some darkened corner of fear could have been his story. But the pit of worry was not for Joseph. That pit is not meant for you either. The pit of worry is like a darkened cave filled with tunnels going off in various directions. Each tunnel ends in a pit of despair. Lingering long in the pit of worry only heaps more worries upon your head. Cast your cares upon the Lord before fear paralyzes you. *"Casting all your care upon Him, for He cares for you."* (1 Peter 5:7) Casting the cares of this life upon Him opens the door of the pit, releasing you out of the pit of worry. Then, you shall enjoy your God-given blessings, rather than singing a song of woes.

Slumped over in a pit of bitterness would have proven destructive for Joseph. But, he refused that pit as well. Walking the road of revenge would have most definitely pulled him from His God ordained and blessed path. Clinging to his wounds, remembering the evil plot of his brothers, would have had him drinking from the poisonous cup of bitterness. The sweetness of God's blessings and the poison of bitterness do not flow from the same cup. Joseph refused to allow his blessings to drown in a cup of bitterness.

Deliverance from the pit took Joseph on a life's journey that he did not expect. In Egypt, he was promoted from the pit to Potiphar's right-hand man. Hate punched his ticket, sending him into Egypt. However, the loving care and divine favor of the Shepherd overruled the hate of his brothers. A poverty-stricken slave, his brothers had envisioned for Joseph. Little did they know that the blessings of God had followed little brother's trail. Instead of living as a pauper, as his brothers intended, Joseph lived in prosperity. *"The Lord was with Joseph, and he was a successful man; and he was in the house of his master the Egyptian."* (Genesis 39:2) His brothers thought they had dictated his destiny, but they had no idea what the future held for them or their brother. Instead of the pit taking him out, it was merely a stepping-stone to his promotion. The pit could not stop the blessings that God had ordained for Joseph.

Life will not always be a scoop of ice cream with a bright red cherry on top. Sometimes, it may seem that you have fallen into a pit with no way out. But if you have never fallen into a pit, you may never understand the deliverance of God. The Shepherd hears your cries from the pit. Just like Joseph, the pit can be used for your deliverance instead of your destruction. Promotion may arise out of the miry pit that seems to be holding you down. Afflictions come, but so does deliverance. *"Many are the afflictions of the righteous, but the Lord deliverers him out of them all."* (Psalm 34:19) Blessings are yours to be had, in spite of the pitfalls that come your way.

Many lessons that are for our good, and not our demise, can be learned when we are sitting in a pit. Often, it is in the pit where lessons are turned into blessings. Prayers prayed from the pit have never gone unnoticed by the Lord. A few times, we probably all have had our sights set upon the door, which we were certain was our way of deliverance. Then suddenly, an unexpected door opened, and our deliverance walked right through. God always comes through the right door and at the right time. Sitting in the bottom of a pit, Joseph probably was not praying that he would be sold into Egypt. God came through at the right time with the right answer.

Trapped in a pit, you may lift up your eyes and see the salvation of the Lord. You can count on Him to protect you in the pit, just as He protected Joseph. At just the right time, He will make a way of escape for you as well. Instead of drowning in your sorrows, allow the pit to become a habitation of praise. A time of intimacy with Christ can be found in the pit. Your faith may arise to a new level, as the Shepherd takes your hand and lifts you out of the pit.

Once again Joseph finds himself as the favored one. Seeing that the Lord was with him, his master promoted Joseph, putting him in charge of his whole house. Even authoritative figures from a strange land saw goodness in Joseph that his brothers did not see.

More importantly, Joseph lived under the divine favor of God. The master's house and all that he had, even the fields, were blessed because of Joseph. What a turn of events—going from a pit, where he was hated, to a position where he is loved and respected.

But the tables turned on Joseph again. Setting her lustful eyes upon handsome Joseph, his master's wife made advances toward him daily. When all of her efforts to seduce Joseph failed, she caught him by his robe, leaving him running out of the house without his garment. Rejecting her advances was the morally right thing for him to do. However, his rejection of her made this lustful woman furious. Setting a trap for Joseph, she falsely accused him of seducing her.

Garment in hand, she had all the evidence that she needed to have Joseph convicted of a crime. Standing without his garment, innocent as could be, poor Joseph was sent to prison. Stripping him of his garment (coat of many colors), his brothers had thrown him in the pit. Being stripped of his garment by this lustful, immoral woman landed him in prison. In both cases, his identity was in his garment. The coat of many colors identified him as the favored son of his father. Likewise, the second garment identified him as Potiphar's servant.

Identifying you as a child of God is the robe of the righteousness of Christ, which He has so lovingly wrapped around you. Your enemy is more infuriated by your majestic robe than Joseph's evil brothers were of his prized coat. Hurling attacks upon you is his game. But rest assured, the deliverer is stronger than the destroyer. *"No weapon formed against you shall prosper."* (Isaiah 54:17) The blood of Jesus must stop any weapon that the enemy hurls your way. No weapon can penetrate through His blood. Stand strong and take authority over the enemy in the name of Jesus.

The blessings of God blew right through those prison walls. The divine favor of God was so mightily upon Joseph that he even found favor with the prison guard. *"But the Lord was with Joseph and showed him mercy, and He gave him favor in the sight of the keeper of the prison."* (Genesis 39:21) No matter where Joseph abode, regardless of situations surrounding him, the blessings of God seem to chase him down. The goodness and mercy of the Lord was with Joseph all the days of his life.

Remember the dreams that Joseph had dreamed—those dreams that sent his brothers into a raging fit? As a prisoner, dreams once again shaped his destiny. Pharaoh's chief baker and butler were thrown into prison with Joseph. One night both the baker and the butler had a different dream. God revealed the interpretation of each dream to Joseph. Within three days, the butler would be released, and the baker would be killed. And it happened just the way Joseph said it would. Joseph had one request of the butler: he asked the butler if he would speak to Pharaoh on his behalf after the butler's release.

Imagine Joseph sitting in that prison day after day, expecting to be released. But the butler forgot all about Joseph until one day Pharaoh had some disturbing dreams that he wanted someone to interpret. Oh then, the butler remembers Joseph, and speaks highly of him to Pharaoh. Finally, they call for Joseph to be released from the dungeon.

Pharaoh's dreams meant that seven good and prosperous years were coming. On the hills of the seven good years would be seven years of severe famine. Pharaoh desperately needed someone to be in charge of managing the food supply during the good years, making it last throughout the bad times. Who better for the job than dear old Joseph? Once again, a big promotion lay in store for the hated brother, the falsely condemned criminal, Joseph. Going from prisoner to the second in command of the land, Joseph stepped out of the dungeon and into a dynasty. He held his position with honor and integrity. He devised a good plan of storing up enough food through the good years to last them throughout the famine.

Just as Joseph had interpreted the dream, when the seven good years ended, there were seven barren years. The famine did not just affect Egypt. Food was in short supply in all other lands, as well. That meant that Joseph's ill-willed, hateful brothers that had done such a detestable thing as to cast him away in a pit, then sell him to the Egyptians, were hungry. Having no food had created a serious crisis for all of the family, including Jacob, his dad.

With nothing else left to do, Jacob reluctantly sent his sons to Egypt to buy food. The day had arrived when Joseph's dreams would be fulfilled. The dreams that his family would bow down and serve him would now come to pass. The lives of them and their entire families were literally in Joseph's hands. He could supply them with food and let them live, or he could let them starve to death. Without charge, he provided food for the same brothers that despised and rejected him. Oh, they offered to pay, but Joseph returned their money. This story line would have had a different outcome if Joseph had curled up in the pit of bitterness, unwilling to forgive those who had wronged him.

God had turned the evil plan that his enemies had against Joseph into good. *"But as for you, you meant evil against me; but God meant it for good, in order to bring it about as it is this day, to save many people alive."* (Genesis 50:20) God turned their evil plan into a good purpose. Blessings came out of the pit.

Life certainly had its ups and downs for Joseph. But the Lord was with him at every bend. From a spoiled young kid to the hated brother, God looked after Joseph. Blessings followed him from the pit to prison, and then to the palace. His enemies could not hold him back from the plan that God had for him. The Lord was truly his shepherd, guiding and protecting him all the way.

Rolls of thunder, bolts of lightning, and crashing waves have you thinking that you will surely drown in a pit of sorrow. Then, the master of the seas speaks a calm into your storm. Suddenly, no more sounds of thunder fill the air. The skies above are clear, and the howling winds cease. Never will you find yourself in a pit too deep that God cannot pull you out—there's no prison cell that He cannot enter. Never mind the pit; stay focused upon the Shepherd. Blessings are headed your way.

CHAPTER 9
Blessed Today

Wake up, wake up, you sleepyhead, a brand-new day lies ahead. Awaken with air in your lungs and blood flowing through your veins; you were blessed before your feet ever hit the floor. Wonders that you did not expect to receive may come your way today. Challenges that you did not anticipate may also lie ahead. Whatever the case may be, you have been blessed with another day. Nothing that you experience today will take the Shepherd by surprise. Enjoy the blessings this day has to offer.

You awoke today to a demonstration of the wondrous glory of God. *"And blessed be His glorious name forever! And let the whole earth be filled with His glory."* (Psalm 72:19) Gazing up into the sky, your eyes are filled with wonder, as the beauty of the morning unfolds. Peeping over the horizon is one glorious, spectacular show, as the golden rays of sunshine spread across the way. Adding glamour to this magnificent scene are the clouds spreading across the sky in all their different shapes and sizes. The morning dew covering your ground is another special gift from above. Listen;

hear the birds singing a lovely melody. Feel the breeze as the breath of God blows in the wind. The beauty of each flower is enhanced by its lovely fragrance. Every raindrop that falls from the sky falls under His command. Each little snowflake is a marvel of His majesty. Simply splendid are all the sights and sounds of His majestic creation! You are blessed to enjoy another day of His wonders.

Better than all the gorgeous sights this day has to offer, you awoke to new mercies of the Lord. *"Through the Lord's mercies we are not consumed, because His compassions fail not. They are new every morning; Great is Your faithfulness."* (Lamentations 3:22-23) As night fades into the dawning of a new day, He embellishes you with a brand-new mercy. Each breath that you breathe, He surrounds you with His unfailing, never-ending love. No matter the sorrows of yesterday, this is a new day. Today, you have awakened to a new hope that can only be found in the care of the Shepherd. Embrace this day with great expectations of good things coming your way. Great is His faithfulness and bountiful are His blessings.

Suppose you had a fabulous day yesterday. Great! Don't become so caught up in the exuberance of yesterday's joys that you miss the blessings of today. Rise up with gratitude in your heart, giving thanks and praise for yesterday's blessings. Excitement shall fill the air with the anticipation of today's goodness. Blessings of today are not served out of yesterday's leftovers. Today is a day that is filled with the knowledge, glory, and splendor of Almighty God. The same hand that guided you yesterday is the same hand that will lead you today. The same Shepherd that provided for you yesterday has provision for you today. Just as He rained showers of blessings upon you yesterday, He surely will rain divine favor upon you today. *"This is the day the Lord has made; we will rejoice and be glad in it."* (Psalm 118:24) As you receive of His blessings today, rejoice and be glad.

On the other hand, perhaps yesterday was a gloomy kind of day. Living in the woes of yesterday will certainly overshadow the blessings of today. Crying a river of tears will not wash away the heartaches of yesterday. Yet, those same tears may hinder your happiness today. You cannot have a bright future while living in a gloomy past.

Today you must press on to higher heights. Up ahead of you are new mountains to climb. *"Brethren, I do not count myself to have apprehended; but one thing I do, forgetting those things which are behind and reaching forward to those things which are ahead, I press toward the goal for the prize of the upward call of God in Christ Jesus."* (Philippians 3:13-14) Paul realized that he had not achieved, obtained, or received all that God had in store for him. Until the day that he reached his highest goal, he would forget the past and press forward. Heaven, his ultimate prize, was up ahead. Like Paul, continually reaching forward will have you thrusting and thriving into new joys.

Speaking of a bad day, the apostle Paul experienced quite a few of them. Being of Jewish descent himself, Paul suffered greatly from his fellow Jewish clan. Opposed to his teachings of Christ, his enemies severely tortured and persecuted Paul. Enduring a beating with thirty-nine stripes did not happen only one time to Paul. The agony of such pain, he suffered five times. Three times he was beaten with rods. He felt the blow of stones as they were hurled his way. Pressing on in times of hunger and thirst, toiling on through weary days, he refused to quit. He would not bow to the whirling attacks of the enemy. Discouragement would not hinder Paul! While imprisoned, Paul wrote many encouraging words to his fellow believers. Yet, in spite of it all, he chose to put those things behind him. His focus was on today, instead of yesterday. The evil plotted against him yesterday, certainly, would not determine his destiny today. The pain that he suffered in the past would not deter him from his present-day blessings.

Putting the past behind him, living in the present, Paul lived a life of contentment. *"Not that I speak in regard to need, for I have learned in whatever state that I am, to be content."* (Philippians 4:11) Hiding under a bramble bush of yesterday, afraid to step out into today's world, only holds one back from receiving the joys of today. Paul refused to allow today's victories to be swallowed up in the sorrows of yesterday. Neither would he allow fear to prevent him from moving forward.

Certainly, there are lessons learned from days gone by that we must never forget. Cherished memories are not to be cast aside. But do not continue to live in yesterday. Follow the example of Paul by leaving yesterday in the past and pressing forward. Moment by moment, stay connected to the here and now.

Camping out in your yesterday keeps you from the destination assigned for you today. Your future lies ahead, not behind you. The Israelites suffered greatly at the hand of the Egyptians. Held in bondage, not allowed to leave Egypt, had been their story for four hundred years. Through plagues and miraculous signs and wonders, God delivered them from bondage. You might say they were delivered from a bad yesterday. But with every stumbling block that they encountered, they yearned for yesterday. "Wish we had stayed in Egypt," would be their reply. Fear of today held them in bondage to yesterday. Only a few days' journey, and they should have reached the Promised Land. This short little journey turned into a forty-year escapade through the wilderness.

A joyous celebration they had after crossing the Red Sea. With music and dancing, they sang a beautiful song of praise. Singing of the goodness of God, His strength, and deliverance, they had quite a worship service. They were not focused on yesterday's struggles; neither were they worried about tomorrow. Living in the moment, they reaped their present-day blessings, and they remained in a state of blessedness until the next problem arose. Oh, how quickly their jubilant praise turned into murmuring and complaining.

Three days of travel found them in a wilderness with no water. Then on to the next stop, a place called Marah, where the water was too bitter to drink. Forgetting the deliverance of the Lord, they blamed

Moses for the dilemma facing them. Onward, they marched until they came to a place, which had twelve wells of water. Waiting at the well for them was a generous supply of water, as the Shepherd once again supplied their need. In the midst of their grumbling, they missed the blessing of peace, joy, and contentment. In their whining state of mind, they lost the blessed assurance of God's miraculous provision.

They went through a testing time. We all will have days that we are put to the test. Everything that God does has a purpose. Even testing days are purposeful. *"In this you greatly rejoice, though now for a little while, if need be, you have been grieved by various trials, that the genuineness of your faith, being much more precious than gold that perishes, though it is tested by fire, may be found to praise, honor, and glory at the revelation of Jesus Christ . . ."* (1 Peter 1:6–7) Rejoice, even when your heart is grieved. Our faith is purified by fire and polished through the testing days. On the days of trials and tears, rejoice. You are still blessed!

Past failures, regrets of former mistakes, maybe even horrible sins may plague your mind with guilt. Laughing all the way, the devil is saying, "Guilty as charged." Condemned is your fate, he would say. Gather up all your past faults, and put them where they belong. In the past, out of your mind, is where they should go. Those were the blunders of yesterday. Today is a new day.

Not guilty is the verdict that Jesus Christ has spoken over His children. *"There is therefore now no condemnation to those who are in Christ Jesus, who do not walk according to the flesh, but according to the Spirit."* (Romans 8:1) Child of God, no matter what sins were in your yesterday, today you stand before your Lord as innocent. The transgressions of your past, He has cast as far as the east is from the west, never to be remembered against you again. Don't go fishing for what Jesus has cast into a sea of forgetfulness.

As Jesus hung upon the cross, two guilty men hung next to him—thieves being put to death for their crimes, one hanging on each side of Christ. One of them turned to Jesus, saying, "Remember me." Jesus quickly assured him that *today*, he would be with Him in paradise. Yesterday he was a criminal; today he was going to be with Jesus in paradise. His fate was not determined by what he did yesterday. Paradise with Jesus was his destiny based on what he did today. Today, he turned to Jesus. Having lived a lifetime under the curse of sin, today he could live a blessed life. Those who had condemned the thief to death did not understand that he had been raised to a new life.

If you have never surrendered your life to Jesus Christ, you may do so today. *"Behold now is the accepted time; behold now is the day of salvation."* (2 Corinthians 6:2) Believe in your heart; confess with your mouth that He is your Lord. *"For with the heart one believes unto righteousness, and with the mouth confession is made unto salvation.* (Romans 10:10) At this very moment, every wrong that you ever committed has been cleansed by the blood of Jesus Christ. In His eyes, your sins never happened. Digging into the past, dragging out your past wrongs only hinders the blessings of today.

Anyone that would like to accept Jesus Christ, as your personal Lord and Savior today, pray this prayer from your heart: Lord Jesus, I know that you shed your blood that my sins may be forgiven. I now repent of all my sins. Thank you for washing and cleansing me. Today, I am making you Lord of my life. In Jesus name.

Anger is another piece of baggage that should be left in your yesterday. It will surely weigh you down today. The longer anger lingers, the heavier the load becomes. *"Be angry, and do not sin": do not let the sun go down upon your wrath."* (Ephesians 4:26) Quickly, get over your anger. Unresolved anger turns into unforgiveness, which then leads to bitterness. A bitter life is not a blessed life. Do not allow yesterday's anger to rob you of today's blessings. Release that anger and be blessed.

Just as living today means letting go of the past, you must also refrain from jumping ahead into the future. Daydreams of tomorrow can swiftly sweep away the joys of today. Hope for tomorrow is wonderful. Fantasizing about things to come can be exciting. Ignoring the blessings of today has been the fate of many while they waited for the next big event to make them happy. While waiting for the pie in the sky of the future, don't miss feasting on the good things of today.

Neither allow your blessings of today to get lost in the worries of tomorrow. Anxieties of tomorrow will certainly snuff out today's peace. Release your burdens unto the Shepherd. Otherwise, pleasures that you could enjoy today will slip away into fear of tomorrow. *"Therefore do not worry about tomorrow, for tomorrow will worry about its own things. Sufficient for the day is its own trouble."* (Matthew 6:34) Worry will never pave the road to a blessed life. Don't allow the dread of tomorrow to drown out the blessings of today.

Many sleepless nights have been spent tossing and turning, worrying about tomorrow. Looking at the clock, the night seemed only to get longer. Each tick of the clock brought to your mind another woe. Every passing minute brought on another round of "what if this" or "what if that." Playing over and over in your head was one scenario after another. All the wrestling in your mind could not conjure up a good solution to life's problems. Then here comes the morning, and the scene that played over and over in your mind all night, never happened.

Chalk that one up to a night that you were robbed. A restful night of sleep was stolen. Anxiousness engulfed your mind, soul, and spirit, robbing you of your peace. Courage gave way to discouragement, stealing your joy. Fear stole your faith, which led to doubt. If the enemy can steal your faith, then you have been stripped of a precious blessing. As you wrestled throughout the night into the wee hours of the morning, you felt downright disheartened. Remember, throughout this horrendous night the Shepherd never left your side.

Planning for your future is different than worrying about tomorrow. While forgetting the past, Paul looked to the future. Pressing onward, with anticipation, he looked ahead. Having a plan in place for tomorrow is wise. However, if your plans become interrupted, do not despair. Should a storm arise today, Jesus will still be the calm in your storm.

Plans that are turned into preparations are prosperous. A great plan may have little value, if the necessary preparations are not carried out. Ants are tiny little creatures, yet very wise. "The ants are a people not strong, yet they prepare their food in the summer." (Proverbs 30:25) Little ants are munching on a meal today because of yesterday's planning. Their food is not gathered up by worrying. The little creatures continue to eat because of the planning and preparation.

All the planning and preparing in the world will not prevent troublesome days from time to time. We have all experienced dark and dreary days. Today, you may have been met with news that seemed to rock your world, shatter all your dreams, and crush your heart. Bleak as your life seems to be, hope still lies at your door. The same God, who carried you on angel wings as you soared to new heights, still has you upon His wingspan. The same God, who gently cradled you in His protective arms as you walked through your darkest valley, still holds you in His loving arms. On the dark, cloudy days that sorrows seem to pour like rain, He will cast a beautiful rainbow across your sky. Keep your eyes upon Him, and watch the blessings come down.

The closing of the day brings on another exhibit of sheer delight. The going down of the sun is just as magnificent as it is when it's rising. Twinkle, twinkle little star! How beautiful you are. The most proficient ballet dancer of all time has never performed an act as graceful as the stars dancing across the sky. The brilliance of the bright shining moon, glowing in the dark, adds a special touch as you close your eyes upon this day. Counting your blessings of the day will surely have you missing a few. Lay your head down in gratitude for each blessing that came your way today. Today you are blessed! Tomorrow is another day!

CHAPTER 10

One Moment With the Shepherd

One moment with the Shepherd changes everything. Lives are instantly changed as they encounter Jesus. A mountain load of troubles may come tumbling down after a good quality moment spent with Him. Miraculously, blinded eyes have been opened, the deaf made to hear, the dumb to talk, and the lame to walk, after a moment in His presence.

After lying thirty-eight long years, unable to walk, a crippled man was totally astonished as, *"Jesus said to him, 'Rise, take up your bed and walk"* (John 5:8) After thirty-eight agonizing years and one moment with the Shepherd, the crippled man took up his bed and walked. He had no physical therapy. Special training teaching him to walk again was not necessary. His legs moved upon the command of Jesus. He was no longer crippled after just one moment with the Shepherd.

Just one moment with the Shepherd may erase a lifetime of pain. Pushing and shoving through the crowded streets, a woman pressed forward, just to have one moment with the Shepherd. All she needed was one quick touch of the hem of His garment. Instantly, she was healed as she reached her hand through the crowd and touched His garment. Relieved from the miserable suffering that had plagued her for twelve long years made all her efforts worthwhile. What a difference one moment with the Shepherd can make!

Touching more than the hem of His garment, she grabbed His attention! Out of all the mob of people, He felt her touch. Countless multitudes of people cover the face of this earth. Yet, the Good Shepherd knows you by name. Reach out toward Him, and you will have His full attention. In the moment that you call upon Him, His eyes are focused upon you. His ears are open to hear your cries. And His hand is outreached toward you. In one moment of time, you may touch Him, and you shall be blessed.

My, how the perspective of life changes when a moment is spent with the Shepherd. From the Shepherd's point of view, things look much differently than through our human eyes. One moment with the Shepherd certainly changed the outlook on life for Zacchaeus. A thief in character and a tax collector by trade defined Zacchaeus. Spurred on by selfishness and greed, he lined his pockets by shady means. Stealing was his game. Gain all the wealth that he could by whatever means necessary was his philosophy. No amount of money could satisfy the longing of his heart. Life through human eyes can never be fulfilled.

But on the day that Jesus came to town, everything changed for Zacchaeus. Too short to see over the crowd, Zacchaeus hurriedly climbed up a tree to get a glimpse of Jesus as He passed his way. As Jesus passed by the tree, He looked up and called Zacchaeus down. "I am going to your house today," said Jesus to Zacchaeus. Quickly, he scurried down that tree as fast as he could. Not only did Zacchaeus get a glance of Jesus, but Jesus noticed him as well.

That one moment of time, when Jesus came by, changed Zacchaeus from the inside out. Gladly, he would give half of all that he had to the poor. All that he had wrongfully taken from anyone, he would restore to them four times more. One moment with the Shepherd turned Zacchaeus from a greedy character to a generous man, a thief to a giver. His encounter with Jesus completely changed his heart and soul. Instead of seeing things through the world's point of view, he caught a vision of the Shepherd's point of view.

No longer did Zacchaeus see his glass as half empty—or should I say—his pockets. Now he saw his pockets full and running over. Years of trying to fill his pockets never brought satisfaction into his life. But one moment with the Shepherd satisfied the longing of his heart. Just one moment with the Shepherd turned a cursed life into a blessed life. Life would never be the same again for Zacchaeus. Life was much sweeter after His moment with the Shepherd.

It seemed to be just an ordinary day for one certain Samaritan woman, who made her usual trip to the well to draw water. Unexpectedly, a gentleman of Jewish descent met her at the well. Much to her surprise, since the Samaritans and the Jews did not mix and mingle together, He asked her to give Him a drink of water. Amazed, she questioned why He, being a Jew, would ask her, a Samaritan woman, for water. She was completely stunned at His answer.

If you only knew who I am, you would ask Me for a drink, Jesus responded. Drink of the water of this well, and you will become thirsty again, He said to her. But, if you would only drink of the water that I have to offer, you will never be thirsty again. Everlasting life springs up from the well of water that I give. "Oh yes", she replied, "give me water from your well." Without hesitation, this Samaritan woman gladly accepted a drink of water from a man who was of the Jewish clan. Suddenly, her customary trip to the well turned into one extraordinary, life-changing day.

She was not known, throughout her region, as a woman of upstanding character. Quite the opposite, she had a rather undesirable reputation. Jesus was not looking for a highly respected person. Certainly, He was not looking for someone who was worthy to drink from His living water. None of us are worthy. We drink of His everlasting water because *He* is worthy! Rather, He was looking for anyone who would accept His offer of the living water that gives eternal life. In one moment, mercy was extended unto her; Grace redeemed her; and His love covered all her sins. One moment with the Shepherd, and she became a new person. Known for a different reason, now a new character defined this woman.

This was the most blessed trip that she had ever made to the well. Going to draw water, and she was drawn unto the Shepherd. She went to the well lost, but Jesus found her. She approached the well in darkness, spiritually blind. One moment with the Shepherd opened her eyes and now she could see. She walked to the well deceived and left knowing Truth! She came away from the well with much more than a pitcher of water. Eternal life was waiting for her at the well. One moment with the Shepherd and her filthy rags of sins were stripped off, and the robe of the righteousness of Christ was draped around her.

Eager to tell others of this new-found water, which was a new-found life, she left her water pot sitting there as she strolled off to share her experience. *"Come, see a Man who told me all things that ever I did. Could this be the Christ?"* (John 4:29) Certainly, she had met Christ. The news was too good to keep to herself. "Come, meet Christ!" is still the call of today.

Any who have not come to this well of living water may freely come and drink. Anyone, who is reading this book right now, who has never come to the well called Jesus Christ, please let this be your defining moment with the Shepherd. Step up to the well with a thirst and hunger in your heart to meet Him. With open arms, He is standing by, waiting to receive you. Now you have received eternal life. One moment with the Shepherd, and your life is instantly changed.

Nothing like a moment with the Shepherd to change a personality. Before his moment with the Shepherd, Saul of Tarsus was quite a scoundrel. Hate for Jesus Christ led him to persecute as many Christians as he could. Wreaking havoc on the church, Saul was responsible for many being thrown into prison, even murdered, because of their belief in Christ. Arresting followers of Christ was his intent as he journeyed to Damascus. You might say, this was one journey that did not go as planned.

Hate spewed out of his heart, as Saul marched down that road with letters in hand from the Jewish high priest, granting the authority to have all Jesus followers arrested. In his eyes, persecution of the Christians was a very worthwhile mission. When bam—right there in the middle of the road, Saul was struck by a blinding light. Upon hearing a voice from heaven, he began to shake and tremble. Jesus asked, *"Saul, Saul, why are you persecuting Me?* (Acts 9:4) Saul experienced Jesus firsthand. This was his moment of conversion.

His moment with the Shepherd changed his life so radically, that his name was changed from Saul to Paul—later to be known as the apostle Paul. His mission to persecute Christians was suddenly changed to a full-blown operation of preaching the gospel to unbelievers. Paul organized churches, preached Jesus Christ to many, and wrote letters of instruction and encouragement to those who followed Christ. This changed man penned many scriptures found in the New Testament today. A heart once filled with hate was now running over with love. Because of his very special moment with the Shepherd, not only did his life change, but it became life changing for many others, as well.

A God moment can appear anytime and anywhere. One lady managed to navigate her way through a busy crowd to have her moment with Him. The crippled man just lay in his bedridden condition while the Shepherd approached him. One woman encountered

Him at the well while another gentleman met Him head-on on the roadway. Probably, few have ever had their moment with the Shepherd down under the deep blue sea, in the belly of a fish, such as Jonah.

Go to Nineveh was the instruction given to Jonah. Not Nineveh, he thought. I will just get myself on a ship and head toward Tarshish, Jonah surmised. So, he bought himself a ticket and off he went, heading the opposite direction of where God had said. As Jonah found out, he could not outrun God, neither could he hide from Him. The Shepherd knew exactly where Jonah was.

The Lord sent a powerful storm, causing great winds and crashing waves. Overtaken by fear, the others onboard cried out to their false gods, to no avail. Knowing that the storm was a direct result of his rebellion, Jonah begged his fellow shipmates to throw him overboard. "Oh no," they replied. They rowed and paddled as hard as they could, trying to reach the shore. When all attempts failed, they tossed Jonah into the water.

Jonah became dinner for one happy fish. That fish swallowed him down in one big gulp. In the belly of that fish, Jonah lay for three full days and nights. The belly of that fish was the designated place for a God moment for Jonah. That Jesus-filled meeting changed Jonah's course. The attitude of "I will not go," had now become, "I will go."

Moments with the Shepherd may quickly turn into hours. Seeking Him may even turn into days, as was the case in the days of Esther. All of the Jews were in great danger; death was lurking at their door. An evil man, Haman, coerced the king to sign a declaration, declaring all Jews to be killed. With the king's ring, this evil decree was signed. The king was ignorant of the fact that his own wife, Esther, was also a Jew.

Mordecai, Esther's cousin, sent word to Esther of the dire state of affairs facing the Jews. He pleaded with her to speak to the king on behalf of her fellow kinfolk. Meanwhile, Mordecai called upon all the Jews in the region to fast and pray, seeking God on their behalf. Three days they went with no food as they prayed, calling upon the Lord. Their moment with the Shepherd turned into days.

However, Esther was not privileged to approach the king at any time she wished. No one, including the Queen, was allowed into the inner court of the king unless he extended the golden scepter unto him or her. She must wait for an opportune moment, to enter into the presence of the king. A moment of invitation was needed.

Dressed in her royal apparel, Esther appeared in the inner court of the king's house while he was seated upon his royal throne. As he spotted his gorgeous wife, the king held up the golden scepter, inviting her to come into the inner court with him. "What can I do for you?" he asked his beautiful wife. Whatever his darling wife requested was his command. Even up to one half of the kingdom, he would have gladly given to her.

Quite pleased she would be if he would attend a banquet that she had prepared. By the way, bring Haman with you, she requested. Not knowing that he was being set up, Haman felt honored to be invited to the Queen's banquet. While they were feasting, Esther requested that they return for another banquet the next day. Haman was so prideful that he almost could not contain himself. Quickly, he rushed home to spread the news to his wife, his children, and friends. I have dined with the king and queen today. Also, I have been invited to feast with them again tomorrow.

But tomorrow was another day, another story. Strutting into the banquet hall, Haman was beside himself as he saw the beautiful banquet table set. About that time, Esther revealed the purpose of the feast, which sent Haman spiraling down off of his pedestal. She exposed his wicked plan to kill all the Jews to her husband, the king. In a furious rage, the king arose and went into his garden palace. While the king was out in the garden, Haman was inside, pleading with Esther for his life. As the king entered back into the palace, Haman was upon Queen Esther's bed, begging for his life to be spared. A possible crime of Haman forcing himself upon his cherished wife was the picture that the king saw.

Previously, Haman had built gallows for the hanging of Mordecai. Death was the sentence that the king handed down to Haman. Justice was served by hanging him on the same gallows that he had built. Haman was dead, and the declaration of death to all Jews was overturned. Numerous lives were spared because Esther had a moment with the earthly king, and Mordecai and the others Jews had moments of time with the Shepherd.

Eternal life has been granted to countless souls because some loved one went into the King's palace and pleaded on their behalf—lifting their name up before the throne of God in a moment of prayer. Unknown are the times that tragedy has been avoided as someone spent a moment offering up a prayer of protection. When destruction could have come, a moment with the Shepherd turned a disaster into a blessing. Moments with the Shepherd turned into days, then weeks, evolving into a lifetime spent in His presence, leading to a blessed life.

CHAPTER 11

In His Presence

Ringing out loud and clear is a constant call to enter into the presence of God. Wow, such an honor and privilege to be called into his presence. Of course, His presence covers the earth. Any place on earth that I go, He is there. No matter how high above the earth that I may soar, your presence will be there. Should I dip down to the deepest part of the sea, there you will be. In the darkest part of the night, I cannot hide from your presence. Since there is no place that His presence does not abide, then how can I be called into His presence? Isn't everyone already in His presence? He is calling out to mankind to experience His presence through a relationship with Him. Are you acquainted with Him, or are you in a relationship with Him? Bidding His sheep to live in His presence is His cry. Live each moment with your spirit connected to Him. Remain aware that He is ever present, right there with you, wherever you are. When you have entered into the realm of enjoying His presence, then you have entered into the place where blessings flow like a flooding river.

Many preparations and much ado must be made before anyone can enter into the presence of royalty. Being welcomed into a royal palace begins with an official invitation. Entrance will be denied to anyone not dressed in proper attire from head to toe. With head held high, stepping inside the palace, you have entered into a place where perfection is demanded. "Mind your manners" has taken on a new meaning. Your every little move is carefully examined, and your behavior is expected to be impeccable. Precisely, my dear, your every word shall be spoken properly. Proper etiquette must be followed at all times, while in the presence of royalty.

Unlike an earthly kingdom, Jesus bids you come to Him just as you are. The invitation has been given. Having not the power nor authority to cleanse self, sinners may come to Him in their dirty, filthy rags of sin. Making the sinner clean is His specialty. Come as you are; He will cleanse your dirty soul. Many souls that once were held as prisoners, ravaged by the evils of this world, have been set free as they responded to His call. Groping along in the darkness of this fallen world, their eyes were opened by the sheer presence of God.

Oh yes, we all have once walked the darkened path that leads to destruction. But as His presence shone a light into many hearts, lives have been changed. The revelation of His glorious splendor takes us into a deeper dimension of life than ever before. Going beyond the things of this earth that will one day pass away, His presence carries us into a heavenly realm.

Recognizing your need for Him, you humbly come. Though you come with a heart bowed in humility, you need not come with head hung low in shame. Unworthy, we all stand before Him. In spite of all our shame, He has beckoned us to come boldly. *"Let us therefore come boldly to the throne of Grace, that we may obtain mercy and find grace to help in time of need."* (Hebrews 4:16) Come; stand in His presence, before His throne with great confidence. In His presence, you may let go of all of your shame. As you respond with an astounding "yes" to His call to come unto Him, all your wrongs are then erased. *"As far as the east is from the west, so far has He removed our transgressions from us."* (Psalm 103:12) A beautiful robe of righteousness has now replaced the garment of sin that you once wore.

In their state of brokenness, the broken and downtrodden may come into His presence. He came to bind up the wounds of the brokenhearted. Pieces of shattered dreams, He has gathered and put back together again. Hearts so broken that duct tape could not fix have been mended in His presence. Discouragement diminishes as courage rises up. The garment of praise strips off the spirit of heaviness.

Like rushing waters flooding over the banks of a mighty river, overwhelming joy shall flood over your soul as you bask in His presence. *"You will show me the path of life; in Your presence is fullness of joy; at Your right hand are pleasures forevermore."* (Psalm 16:11) Certainly most all people have enjoyed moments of happiness. Many times, those happy moments have quickly turned into unhappy ones. Happenings may determine your happiness. In an instant, circumstances can turn your laughter into tears. But He will turn your mourning into dancing. Joy is not connected to your circumstance; joy is attached to your relationship with Jesus Christ. Dwelling in His presence keeps you singing a song of praise, regardless of circumstances.

Joy never ceases, as you abide in His presence. Therefore, you shall continually arise with new strength. *"The joy of the Lord is your strength."* (Nehemiah 8:10) You will accomplish things that previously you had deemed impossible as the supernatural strength of the Lord sweeps over you. *"I can do all things through Christ who strengthens me."* (Philippians 4:13) Lingering in the presence of the Lord increases spiritual strength, just as a person committed to a daily routine of vigorous exercise becomes physically stronger. In His presence, the weak become strong. Commit yourselves to living in His divine presence. As joy bubbles up within your soul, new strength shall continually arise within your spirit.

No wonder, His sheep joyfully enter into His presence with thanksgiving. *"Make a joyful shout to the Lord, all you lands! Serve the Lord with gladness: come before His presence with singing. Know that the Lord, He is God; it is He who has made us, and not we ourselves; we are His people and the sheep of His pasture. Enter into His gates with thanksgiving, and into His courts with praise. Be thankful to Him, and bless His name. For the Lord is good; His mercy is everlasting, and His truth endures to all generations."* (Psalm 100:1–5) Entering into His presence with an awareness of His goodness and mercy will put praise in your heart and a joyful song upon your lips.

In His presence, Adam and Eve heard the voice of God. *"And they heard the sound of the LORD God walking in the garden in the cool of the day, and Adam and his wife hid themselves from the presence of the LORD God among the trees of the garden."* (Genesis 3:8) Sin made them fearful of the presence of God. If we can only hide from His voice, surely then, we can hide from His presence, they thought. His voice was an element of His presence. Sin stole their peace. Their response to His presence robbed them of their joy. Therefore, they became weak instead of strong, fearful instead of faithful.

Dear friend, no need to be fearful of His presence. "Oh, but I have sinned!" you exclaim. Well, join the crowd. So have the rest of us. *"If we confess our sins, He is faithful and just to forgive us our sins and to cleanse us from all unrighteousness."* (John 1:9) Recognizing your sin opens the doorway, leading to confession, repentance, and forgiveness. Unlike fear, faith draws you into His presence, instead of running from His presence, as Adam and Eve did.

The presence of God appeared unto Moses in the midst of a burning bush. As His voice called out to Moses, "Here am I" was the reply given by Moses. Boldly, Moses stood in the presence of God and bravely responded to His call. Like Adam and Eve, Moses had experienced the presence of God by hearing His voice. But, oh, what a different response.

In His presence, His sheep are empowered. The task at hand was not easy for Moses. However, standing at the bush, in the very presence of God, he was empowered to carry out his God-given duties. As you wait in His presence, you too are empowered. *"But ye shall receive power when the Holy Spirit has come upon you: and you shall be witnesses to Me both in Jerusalem, and in all Judea and Samaria, and to the end of the earth."* (Acts 1:8) Better to stand in His presence and be endued with power, than to stand powerless in the face of your enemy.

Peace abounds in the presence of God. Not every situation that you encounter will be a peaceful event. But in the midst of turmoil, peace may surround you, as you are engulfed in His presence. A mind focused on problems is a troubled mind. Shifting focus from problem to the problem solver soothes the troubled soul. Wandering minds that wander from the presence of God will experience a wandering peace that wavers in and out. As your mind goes back and forth, so does your peace. *"You will keep him in perfect peace, whose mind is stayed on You, because he trusts in You."* (Isaiah 26:3) Those who keep their mind upon the Lord will continually live in peace. Peace that the world cannot give, therefore the world cannot understand. Peace which cannot be explained or understood can only be found in the presence of God.

In His presence, you are sheltered under His protective wing. *"He who dwells in the secret place of the Most High shall abide under the shadow of the Almighty."* (Psalm 91:1) Gathering her young underneath her wings, a mother bird stands guard against any prey that would harm her babies. But then, along comes some huge vulture, overpowering the helpless mother, devouring her young. In the presence of God, you stand under a power that cannot be shaken. He is greater than all other powers that would come against you. *"No weapon formed against you shall prosper."* (Isaiah 54:17) He has the power to break every chain and demolish every weapon that would rise up against you. You are sheltered safely in His arms. *"He shall cover you with His feathers, and under His wings you shall take refuge; His truth shall be your shield and buckler."* (Psalm 91:4)

Standing in His presence, all hope is never lost. He is the creator of hope. Christ, the hope of glory, which lives within you, is a constant companion. Surrounded by His presence in your loneliest hours, He comforts you. His shoulders are big and wide enough for you to cry a river of tears. With each teardrop that He wipes from your eyes, a new hope arises. Today may find you in a destitute place. Desperate for answers, you search here and there, high and low. Answers are nowhere to be found. Seemingly, no good thing can come from where you are right now. The greatest hope for all the world came from a place that was not expected to yield any good thing.

Nothing good was expected to come from the city of Nazareth. *"Can anything good come out of Nazareth?"* (John 1:46) But oh, what came out of Nazareth! Jesus Christ came from this city that had been deemed by mankind as a hopeless place. Hope for all the world was conceived in a place where no hope was expected to be found. The presence of God had come to Nazareth. His presence turns hopelessness into hope, sorrows into joy, and curses into blessings. Because of the hope that came out of Nazareth, there is hope for you right here and right now.

His presence is glorious. A mighty worship service took place upon the completion of the temple, built by King Solomon. The holy vessels were set in place; musicians came with their instruments, and singers lifted their voices, praising and magnifying the Lord. A thick cloud of the presence of God filled the entire place as they worshiped. In the midst of their praise, an explosion of His glory erupted, filling the atmosphere. The glorious presence of God was so mightily upon the priest that they could not even stand.

The temple now resides in the heart of every born-again believer. As we set our hearts upon worship to Him, we too may enjoy the awesome greatness of His glorious presence. As we stand in awe of Him, we shall experience His majesty. The breath of His presence breathed upon us, makes the atmosphere around us glorious.

More numerous than all the grains of sand upon the seashore are the bountiful blessings that abound in His presence. Reach as high as you may, dig as deep as you can, and you will never come to the end of His blessings. Only in His presence can you live the abundant life that He came to give.

CHAPTER 12

The Broken Veil

God created a perfect world and a perfect people. Living in paradise, Adam and Eve enjoyed fellowship with God. The human race was created to have communion with God. Living in His presence was His plan for mankind from the beginning. Everything was good until the sly, old deceiver, Satan, came along with his deceptive scheme. Falling into temptation, Adam and Eve committed the first sin, which tainted the world and corrupted the entire human race. Consequently, all people from that day forward were born with a sinful nature. Since God, in His holy nature, cannot dwell with sin, the relationship between God and man was broken.

Satan did not care about the fruit that he convinced Eve to eat. Destroying the God-man relationship was his full intent. Being cast out of heaven because of his sinful pride, he fully understood that sin could not abide in the presence of Almighty God. The sly old fox underestimated God—because God had a plan to redeem mankind back into relationship with Him. Therefore, He sent His Son, Jesus Christ, to redeem mankind from his sins, thereby, restoring man's relationship with God.

Preventing the common folk from entering the holy of holies (the most holy place), a solid veil hung in the temple. The sinful nature of man held them on the other side of the curtain. The hanging veil was a staunch reminder that sinful people were not allowed in the holy presence of God. The broken relationship between God and man, which sin had caused, was vividly demonstrated in that one solid curtain.

Going beyond the veil, into the most Holy place, was off limits to anyone except the High Priest. A rigid process of cleansing and purification was required before he entered. He was only allowed beyond the veil once a year for the purpose of making atonement for the sins of the people. Most certainly, an acceptable blood sacrifice was required before he entered into the holy of holies. *"And without shedding of blood there is no remission."* (Hebrews 9:22)

Hanging on the cross, as Jesus breathed His last breath, the veil was split into two pieces. *"And Jesus cried with a loud voice, and breathed His last. Then the veil of the temple was torn in two from top to bottom."* (Mark 15:37–38) The torn veil signified that a new order had been set in motion. A new covenant was established. A blood covenant made from the blood of a spotless lamb had redeemed mankind. Not one more drop of blood ever needed to be shed again. Man was no longer prohibited from entering into the presence of the living God.

THE BROKEN VEIL

The broken veil represented that the Holy Presence of God is now available to all who will come. Since no other blood is worthy enough or sufficient enough to cover all the sins of the world, His blood became the ultimate sacrifice for all time, restoring the God-man relationship. *"For Christ also suffered once for sins, the just for the unjust, that **He might bring us to God**, being put to death in the flesh but made alive by the Spirit."* (1 Peter 3:18) His death split the veil in two and gave mankind constant access into the wondrous presence of God.

Instead of a veil standing before mankind, separating man from the holy presence of God, now a door leading into His divine presence stands before man. Speaking with great authority, Jesus said, *"I am the door of the sheep."* (John 10:7) Back in those days, the sheep were held in pens across the pasturelands. Only one gate allowed the shepherd entrance into the pen to care for the sheep. The same is true of the doorway called Jesus. He is the only access to God, the Father. Another powerful statement made by Jesus, *"I am the way, the truth, and the life. No one comes to the Father except through Me."* (John 14:6) Trying to enter into the presence of Almighty God through another door, except Jesus, will lead straight down a road called deception.

A veil torn into pieces meant never again would an earthly High Priest make atonement for the sins of man. Jesus Christ became the High Priest. *"Therefore, in all things He had to be made like His brethren, that He might be a merciful and faithful High Priest in things pertaining to God, to make propitiation (reconciliation) for the sins of the people."* (Hebrews 2:17) In His role of High Priest, He extends mercy like no other High Priest could. He is faithful to bring reconciliation between God and man. All who come to Him, believing that He is the Son of God, the Redeemer, the High Priest, now may have their sins forgiven, be washed by His blood, and be reconciled back into fellowship with God.

The old system failed to reach perfection in that it could never reconcile sinners back to God. Year after year, the High Priest made atonement for their sins. Yet they still could never go beyond the veil into the most holy place. The yearly atonement made on behalf of the people could never bridge the gap between God and man. Neither could access into His glorious presence be gained by laws and rituals.

The perfect lamb shed His blood, redeeming the sinful man, and restoring the God-man relationship. We do not come to Him through strict rules and regulations, called religion. Neither do we come through an earthly man, such as the High Priest of old days. Relationship with Jesus connects us to the holy presence of God.

Before the veil was torn, all who ever came as High Priest were of the earthly nature. You might say, they too were bound by a sinful nature. But now Christ has come from a heavenly kingdom. *"Seeing then that we have a great High Priest who has passed through the heavens, Jesus the Son of God, let us hold fast our confession. For we do not have a High Priest who cannot sympathize with our weaknesses, but was in all points tempted as we are, yet without sin."* (Hebrews 4:14-15) He has ascended into heaven, seated upon a heavenly throne, making Him the perfect, spotless High Priest. While He was totally God, He also had lived upon this earth in a fleshly body. Unlike the earthly priest, He clearly understands our weak points. He now sits at the right hand of God, making intercession for you and me.

The dividing veil made way for open communication between God and man. In days gone by, God spoke through prophets. *"God, who at various times and in various ways spoke in time past to the fathers by the prophets, has in these last days spoken to us by His Son, whom He has appointed heir of all things, through whom also He made the worlds;"* (Hebrews 1:1-2) For an example, God spoke to Moses, not to the whole tribe of the Israelites. As mediator between God and man, Moses spoke to the people. Jesus Christ is our mediator *"For there is one God and one Mediator between God and men, the Man Christ Jesus."* (1 Timothy 2:5) No other mediator can connect you to God. Through Christ, we have access to hear the voice of God and to pour our heart out unto Him, knowing that He hears when we call upon Him.

As the veil was split, Grace walked right through! Grace is a gift of which we are so unworthy and undeserving to receive. The filthy, sinful nature of man could never deserve entrance into the throne of God. But His Amazing Grace paved the way, opened the door, and ushered us right into His presence. *"For by grace you have been saved through faith, and that not of yourselves; it is the gift of God."* (Ephesians 2:8) Because of the blood of Jesus, we now live under Grace.

Grace blesses us with the divine favor of God. Sin still cannot enter into the presence of God, but Grace can! Grace has erased our imperfections. God looks beyond the brokenness of our human nature and sees us clothed in His Righteousness by His Grace!

Undeniably, Grace is not a written permission slip to continue living a sinful life. Temptation may continually knock on your door. But instead of being overcome with sin, Grace empowers the believer to overcome temptation. By His Grace, the Holy Spirit is our helper, strengthening the weak to be made strong. Oh yes, we all will fall short of the mark from time to time. *"For all have sinned and fall short of the glory of God."* (Romans 3:23) Rest assuredly, our faltering ways are never caused by a lack of Grace; our own shortcomings are a result of our failure to resist temptation. Thank God for His redeeming Grace when we do fail to obey.

Brokenness cursed mankind. A broken command of God cursed the world. The curse of sin caused a broken relationship, whereas mankind could not enter into the most holy presence of God. Quite frankly, separation from God causes broken lives. This brokenness was a heartbreak to God. Satan could not keep the entire human race separated from the presence of God forever.

Thankfully, the Good Shepherd turned the curse of brokenness into a blessing of brokenness. Blessed because the curse of sin has been broken off of everyone who is safely in the sheepfold of the Shepherd. By His great power, chains of bondage have been broken, setting the captive free. We are blessed as our own will is broken in total surrender to Him. The broken veil has restored the God-man relationship. Through brokenness, the devil plotted an evil curse upon the world. By means of brokenness, God has blessed mankind. You may now walk right through the broken veil and enter into the most precious relationship ever known to man.

Blessings from the Shepherd can never be numbered. We shall forever be grateful for all our daily needs that He has provided. More times than we would even know, He has guided us upon the mountaintops and led us through the valleys. Surely, He has mended broken fences in our lives. A few He probably mended before we even knew they were broken. He is and forever shall be our provider, protector, defender, and the rock of our salvation. He has sheltered us from storms that we never saw coming. You may have been blessed with great health. Maybe even great wealth has come your way. But blessed to live in His presence far exceeds all the other blessings of life. Blessed are those who know the Shepherd as their Lord.

The LORD bless you and keep you:
The LORD make His face shine upon you,
and be gracious to you:
The LORD lift up His countenance upon you,
and give you peace.

(Numbers 6:24–26)

All scripture is New King James Version.